K Hunter

T 890

GO DOWN, MOSES

The Miscegenation of Time

TWAYNE'S MASTERWORK STUDIES

Robert Lecker, General Editor

GO DOWN, MOSES

The Miscegenation of Time

Arthur F. Kinney

TWAYNE PUBLISHERS
An Imprint of Simon & Schuster Macmillan
New York

PRENTICE HALL INTERNATIONAL
London • Mexico City • New Delhi • Singapore • Sydney • Toronto

Twayne's Masterwork Series No. 148

Go Down, Moses: The Miscegenation of Time
Arthur F. Kinney

Twayne Publishers
An Imprint of Simon & Schuster Macmillan
1633 Broadway
New York, New York 10019-6785

Library of Congress Cataloging-in-Publication Data

Kinney, Arthur F., 1933–
    Go down, Moses : the miscegenation of time / Arthur F. Kinney.
        p.   cm.—(Twayne's masterwork studies ; no. 148)
    Includes bibliographical references and index.
    ISBN 0-8057-8368-7 (cloth).—ISBN 0-8057-8572-8 (pbk.)
    1. Faulkner, William, 1897–1962. Go down, Moses. 2. Afro-Americans in
literature.   3. Race relations in literature.   4. Miscegenation in literature.
    5. Mississippi—In literature.   6. Lynching in literature.   7. Time in literature.
    I. Title.   II. Series.
PS3511.A86G6349   1996
813'.52—dc20   95-52740
                                                                                          CIP

10 9 8 7 6 5 4 3 2 1 (hc)
10 9 8 7 6 5 4 3 2 1 (pb)

Printed in the United States of America

For Lynn Z. Bloom and in memory of Francis Lee Utley and for Emma Nogrady Kaplan and in memory of Sidney Kaplan

When Israel was in Egypt's land,
    Let my people go.
Oppressed so hard they could not stand,
    Let my people go.

We need not always weep and mourn,
    Let my people go.
And wear these slav'ry chains forlorn,
    Let my people go.

The devil thought he had us fast,
    Let my people go.
But we thought we'd break his chains at last,
    Let my people go.

Thus saith the Lord, bold Moses said,
    Let my people go.
If not I'll smite your first born—dead,
    Let my people go.

No more shall they in bondage toil,
    Let my people go.
Let them come out with Egypt's spoil,
    Let my people go.

When Israel out of Egypt came,
    Let my people go.
And left the proud oppressive land,
    Let my people go.

O 'twas a dark and dismal night,
    Let my people go.
When Moses led the Israelites,
    Let my people go.

The Lord told Moses what to do,
    Let my people go.
To lead the children of Israel thro',
    Let my people go.

As Israel stood by the water side,
    Let my people go.
By God's command it did divide,
    Let my people go.

When they reached the other shore,
    Let my people go.
They sang a song of triumph o'er,
    Let my people go.

Chorus.
    Go down, Moses,
    'Way down in Egypt's land.
    Tell ole Pharaoh,
    Let my people go.

—Traditional Negro Spiritual

To talk about Faulkner [on your campus] without talking about race is like talking about an apple pie without the apples.
　　　　—Robert Penn Warren to Chancellor John Davis Williams,
　　　　　　　　　　　—University of Mississippi, 1963

Almost as color defines vision itself, race shapes the cultural eye— what we do and do not notice, the reach of empathy and the alignment of response.
　　　　—Taylor Branch, *Parting the Waters,* 1988

Contents

William Faulkner and his gardener, Andra Price, at Rowan Oak, June 1962.
Copyright © Ed Meed, 1962

Note on the References
and Acknowledgments

The problem of the twentieth century is the problem of the color-line.
—W. E. B. DuBois, 1903

Nearly 400 years after the first African came ashore at Jamestown—and 40 years after Rosa Parks launched the Montgomery bus boycott—Americans are still preoccupied with race. Race divides us, defines us and in a curious way unites us—if only because we still think it matters. Race-based thinking permeates our law and policy, and the sense of racial grievance, voiced by blacks and whites alike, infects our politics. Blacks cleave to their role as history's victims; whites grumble about reverse discrimination. The national mood on race, as measured by *Newsweek*'s latest poll, is bleak: 75 percent of whites—and 86 percent of blacks—say race relations are "only fair" or "poor."

But the world is changing anyway. By two other measures in the same *Newsweek* Poll—acceptance of interracial marriage and the willingness to reside in mixed-race neighborhoods—tolerance has never been higher. The nation's racial dialogue, meanwhile, is changing so rapidly that the familiar din of black-white antagonism seems increasingly out of date.
—Tom Morganthau, *Newsweek,* February 13, 1995

This is the sixth book in which I have published my ideas about the meaning and significance of *Go Down, Moses*; it is that kind of book—powerful, indelible, important, and inescapable. Each time I read it, teach it, or discuss it, I see new meanings and find new rewards, despite the fact that it remains (for me, anyway) Faulkner's most recalcitrant novel. *The Sound and the Fury, As I Lay Dying, Light in August, and Absalom, Absalom!* (all subjects of studies in this series) juxtapose multiple and discordant narrative perceptions of events, yet each of those novels has an indisputable center of gravity, a master narrative, that finally unfolds on Easter Sunday, or in a family's arrival at Jefferson, or with the death of Joe Christmas and the birth of Lena Grove's child, or through debate in a Harvard dormitory room, buttressed by a visit to Sutpen's Hundred. But there is no single overriding narrative that sustains all of *Go Down, Moses* and so coalesces its multiple episodes and viewpoints. And, given the novel's various settings—wilderness, plantation, town—there is no single issue (such as the fall of the house of Compson or the mystery of why Henry Sutpen shot Charles Bon). This makes *Go Down, Moses,* as Faulkner's biographer David Minter has noted, eminently reader-centered (187–88). It gives all of us the opportunity to enter a fictional world made just for us, where meaning is our own. *Go Down, Moses* is not merely a novel that possesses you; it is a novel you must possess for yourself.

Of all Faulkner's novels, this one not only speaks about Southern culture but reaches out to probe American culture as well—not simply our history but also our values, our choices, and our actions. *Go Down, Moses* constantly tests us. When the novel first appeared, Lionel Trilling remarked that "more convincingly than anything [he had] read" it examined "the complex tragedy of the South's racial dilemma," but then went on to add that "its depth and its complication go beyond what committees and commissions can conceive, beyond even the most liberal 'understanding' and the most humanitarian 'sympathy.'"[1] In raising profoundly basic issues about American institutions and American life (and not just in the South), the novel invites us to think of what it means to be American (whether we are or not)—and it becomes extraordinarily urgent in doing so.

I have now lived in Oxford, Mississippi, on more than a dozen occasions, and I still find it difficult to understand the permutations of class, caste, and race in which *Go Down, Moses* is grounded. Take

Note on the References and Acknowledgments

Faulkner's final thought on the book (see chronology), the dedication of it to his model for Molly Beauchamp:

TO MAMMY
CAROLINE BARR
Mississippi
[1840–1940]
Who was born in slavery and who
gave to my family a fidelity without
stint or calculation of recompense
and to my childhood an immeasur-
able devotion and love

What does this really mean? That the book is primarily meant for, or about, blacks? That blacks are the Southern representatives of servitude (mandatory under slavery; freely chosen after emancipation)? That Caroline Barr, as surrogate mother, gave Faulkner what his own white family did not or could not? That whatever else she was to him, Caroline Barr remained, essentially, his (a) "mammy"? Perhaps all of these, combining deep devotion, loyalty, and a sense of place. Whatever the meaning(s) of the dedication, though, it unarguably makes *Go Down, Moses* the most personal of Faulkner's works. To understand this novel is to understand much of its author, too. As I said, the rewards for reading this book are several and special.

The text I cite throughout is the most accessible—the paperback Vintage International edition of *Go Down, Moses* that was first published in 1990. Other citations refer to works listed in the bibliography, and various other sources are mentioned in the notes and references. This book could not have been conceived, much less written, without the splendid biography by Joseph Blotner and his editions of Faulkner's letters and uncollected stories, or the texts of Faulkner's essays and interviews (see bibliography). In addition, a good many previous scholars and critics have been especially helpful. I have drawn on Michel Gresset's chronology of Faulkner and Meredith Smith's chronology of events in *Go Down, Moses* (see Appendix I) for my own; in addition, I have come to learn much from L. D. Brodsky, Michael Grimwood, Daniel Hoffman, Elizabeth Kerr, John T. Matthews, Michael Millgate,

David Minter, Noel Polk, James A. Snead, Eric J. Sundquist, Walter Taylor, Joan Williams, and Joel Williamson. For the past two decades, the residents and scholars of Oxford, Mississippi, have been generous with their time and insights, and I wish to thank publicly, among others, Ann Abadie, Katherine Chandler Andrews, Howard Bahr, Frank Childrey, Jr., Alan and Ann Cochet, Martha Cofield, J. M. Faulkner, Ethel Ferguson, William Ferris, Cheri Friedman, Evans Harrington, Sidney Johnson, Will Lewis, Sr., and Will Lewis, Jr., Ed Meeck, Bill Plunk, Guy Turnbow, Thomas Verich, and Patricia Young, as well as the officers of the Skipwith Historical and Genealogical Society and the local chapters of the Daughters of the American Revolution and the United Daughters of the Confederacy. Finally, I want to thank Lewis DeSimone and Robert Lecker for their faith that this time I'd come closer to getting things right, and my editors at Twayne, Carol Leach and Margaret Dornfeld, who have saved me from error and infelicity and helped in this book's design.

Chronology

1540	Between 20,000 to 30,000 Chickasaw and Choctaw Indians living in what is now Mississippi. (Sam Fathers is part Chickasaw.)
1814	Indians forced to cede their land to Federal government 9 August; it is divided into Mississippi (1817) and Alabama (1819).
1832	King Ishtehotopah agrees, in Treaty of Pontotoc, to leave Mississippi for western lands (largely Oklahoma).
1836	Lafayette County, Mississippi, created, bounded on north in part by Tallahatchie River and south in part by Yocona (formerly Yoconapatafa) River; will serve Faulkner as model for his Yoknapatawpha County.
1897	William Cuthbert Falkner born 25 September to Murry C. and Maud Butler Falkner on Jefferson Street, New Albany, Mississippi (family will move to Ripley in 1898 and to Oxford in fall of 1902).
1918	Author changes spelling of surname to *Faulkner* when he begins work for Winchester Repeating Arms Company in New Haven, Connecticut. Uses new spelling when reporting for duty in Canadian Royal Air Force in Toronto 9 July.
1919	First uses new spelling of name to sign a literary work ("L'Apres-Midi d'un Faune," a poem published in the *New Republic*) on 6 August.
1922	The *Mississippian* publishes "The Hill," his first work set in rural country to become Yoknapatawpha, on 10 March.
1924	Publishes first book, *The Marble Faun* (poems), 15 December.
1925	Publishes "Sunset" (first fiction about a black) in New Orleans *Times-Picayune*, 24 May.

1926	Publishes *Soldiers' Pay* (first novel) with Boni and Liveright in 2,500 copies, 25 February.
1927	Publishes *Mosquitoes* with Boni and Liveright, 30 April.
1929	Publishes *Sartoris* (abridged by Ben Wasson from *Flags in the Dust*) with Harcourt, Brace, in 1,990 copies, 31 January. Publishes *The Sound and the Fury* with Jonathan Cape and Harrison Smith in 1,789 copies, 7 October; first real critical success.
1930	Publishes "A Rose for Emily" in *The Forum*, 30 April; first story in a national magazine. Publishes *As I Lay Dying* with Cape and Smith in 2,522 copies, 6 October. In accepting Nobel Prize for Literature on 12 December, Sinclair Lewis commends Faulkner, who has "freed the South from hoop-skirts."
1931	Publishes revised text of *Sanctuary* with Cape and Smith in 2,219 copies, 9 February; first best-selling work. Publishes *These 13* (stories) with Cape and Smith in 1,928 copies, 21 September; includes "A Justice," about Sam Fathers's ancestry.
1932	Publishes *Light in August* with Harrison Smith and Robert Haas, 6 October.
1933	Publishes *A Green Bough* (poems) with Smith and Haas, 20 April.
1934	Publishes "A Bear Hunt" in *Saturday Evening Post*, 10 February. Publishes *Doctor Martino and Other Stories* with Smith and Haas, 16 April.
1935	Writes agent Morton Goldman 18 February, refusing offer (from *Vanity Fair*?) to write article on lynching: "Tell them I never saw a lynching and so couldn't describe one" (cf. "Pantaloon in Black"). Publishes *Pylon* with Smith and Haas, 25 March. Publishes "Lion" in *Harper's*, December (later expanded and revised for incorporation into *Go Down, Moses*).
1936	Publishes *Absalom, Absalom!* with Random House in 6,000 copies and limited edition of 300 more, 26 October.
1937–1938	Purchases Bailey's Woods, adjacent to his home in Oxford, and Greenfield Farm (model for McCaslin plantation), becoming a large landowner like L. Q. C. McCaslin.
1938	Publishes *The Unvanquished*, 15 February.
1939	Elected to National Institute of Arts and Letters, 18 January. Publishes *The Wild Palms* with Random House, 19 January. Agent Harold Ober receives "The Old People," 3 October.
1940	Ober receives "A Point of Law," 4 January; later revised for "The Fire and the Hearth" in *Go Down, Moses*. Caroline Barr,

to whom *Go Down, Moses* is dedicated (model for Molly Beauchamp), dies 31 January at Rowan Oak, Faulkner's home; he gives funeral sermon. Ober receives "Gold Is Not Always," 19 February; later part of "The Fire and the Hearth" (part 1 only, as separate story), 23 February. Ober receives "Pantaloon in Black," 18 March. Publishes *The Hamlet* with Random House, 1 April. Faulkner writes Haas 3 May, "Ober has four stories about niggers. I can build onto them, write some more, make a book like *The Unvanquished,* could get it together in six months, perhaps." Faulkner writes Haas 27 May, "What a hell of a time we are facing. I got my uniform out the other day. . . . Maybe the watching of all this coming to a head for the last year is why I cant write, dont seem to want to write, that is" (cf. opening conversation in "Delta Autumn"). Haas advances Faulkner $2,400 on *Go Down, Moses* in June. Publishes "A Point of Law" in *Collier's,* 22 June. In July revises "Almost" (later retitled "Was"); sends "Go Down, Moses" directly to *Saturday Evening Post* (it is rejected). In August *Harper's* buys "Pantaloon in Black" for $400. In September publishes "The Old People" in *Harper's*; *Atlantic Monthly* buys "Gold Is Not Always"; *Collier's* buys "Go Down, Moses." In October publishes "Pantaloon in Black" in *Harper's*; not hearing from RAF, Faulkner teaches navigation and radio operation to volunteers in Mississippi. In November publishes "Gold Is Not Always" in *Atlantic Monthly.* In December Ober receives "Delta Autumn" (after November hunting trip in Delta).

1941   Publishes "Go Down, Moses" in *Collier's,* 25 January. In May resumes work on combining stories for *Go Down, Moses* but has not yet thought of uniting them by way of a new part 4 of "The Bear." Haas receives chapter 1 of "The Fire and the Hearth," 5 June. Haas receives part 1 of "The Bear," 25 July. Haas receives part 2 of "The Bear," 9 September. Faulkner sends parts 1, 2, 3, and 5 of "The Bear" to Ober to sell as short story, 27 October. Haas receives part 3 of "The Bear," 9 November. Faulkner sells "The Bear" to *Saturday Evening Post* on 14 November for $1,000; agrees to revise ending. Writes Haas 2 December, "My promise re mss. Dec. 1 is already broken. There is more meat in it than I thought, a section now that I am going to be proud of and which requires careful writing and rewriting to get it exactly right. I am at it steadily" (referring to part 4 of "The Bear," the last part of *Go Down, Moses* written). In mid-December Faulkner sends Random House 121 typed pages with instructions, "DON'T CHANGE EITHER

THE PUNCTUATION OR THE CONSTRUCTION";
expands "Delta Autumn"; requests that "Go Down, Moses" be
put at end of novel and that its title also be used as book's title.

1942   Sends dedication (to Mammy Callie) to Haas, 21 January.
Publishes "The Bear" (without part 4) in *Saturday Evening
Post*, 9 May. Publishes *Go Down, Moses and Other Stories*
with Random House, 11 May (complains to Haas on 26
January 1949, prior to publication of second edition, to omit
and Other Stories: "Moses is indeed a novel.") *Story* publishes
"Delta Autumn" in May-June issue for payment of $25.

1945   Writes to Richard Wright 11 September, "I think that you will
agree that the good lasting stuff comes out of one individual's
imagination and sensitivity to and comprehension of the suffering of Everyman, Anyman, not out of the memory of his
own grief."

1946   Publishes *The Portable Faulkner*, edited by Malcolm Cowley,
with Viking, 29 April; they agree to include "A Justice,"
"Was," "The Bear," and "Delta Autumn" to represent years
1820, 1859, 1883, and 1940, respectively, in chronicle of
Yoknapatawpha County.

1948   Publishes *Intruder in the Dust*, 18 October; the racial theme
raises protests. Elected to American Academy of Arts and
Letters, 24 November.

1949   Writes Haas January 26, "If you will permit me to say so at this
late date, nobody but Random House seemed to labor under
the impression that GO DOWN, MOSES should be titled 'and
other stories.' I remember the shock (mild) I got when I saw the
printed title page. I say, reprint it, call it simply GO DOWN,
MOSES, which was the way I sent it to you 8 years ago." In
spring Hollywood films *Intruder in the Dust* in Oxford;
Faulkner helps to rework final scene of script. *Intruder in the
Dust* premieres at Lyric Theater in Oxford, 11 October.
Publishes *Knight's Gambit* with Random House, 27 November.
In Stockholm, Faulkner loses Nobel Prize by vote of 15 to 3
(vote must be unanimous).

1950   Faulkner publishes letter outside Oxford, in Memphis *Commercial Appeal* on 26 March, protesting simple prison sentence
of Leon Turner, convicted in Mississippi of killing three black
children. Publishes second letter 9 April. In June awarded
Howells Medal for distinguished work in American fiction by
American Academy of Arts and Letters. Publishes *Collected
Stories of William Faulkner* with Random House, 21 August;

includes "A Bear Hunt" and "A Justice." Unanimously elected, with Bertrand Russell, to receive Nobel Prize for Literature, 10 November.

1951	Receives National Book Award for *Collected Stories* in March. Receives French Legion of Honor, 25 May. Publishes *Requiem for a Nun,* 27 September.
1952	Addresses 5,000 members and guests of the Delta Council in Cleveland, Mississippi, on matters of race, 15 May.
1954	Publishes *The Faulkner Reader* with Random House, 1 April; includes "The Bear" (all five parts). In April publishes semiautobiographical essay "Mississippi" in *Holiday.* Publishes *A Fable* with Random House, 2 August.
1955	Signs contract for a collection of hunting stories (*Big Woods*), 21 January. Receives National Book Award for *A Fable* 25 January. *Go Down, Moses* published in Modern Library 11 March. Publishes four letters in Memphis *Commercial Appeal* (20 March; 3, 10, 17 April) arguing for integration of public schools, noting it is absurd "to raise additional taxes to establish another system at best only equal to that one which is already not good enough." Is opposed by friends, neighbors, and relatives, including his brother John. On 12 June writes Else Jonnson in Sweden, "We have much tragic trouble in Mississippi now about Negroes. . . . Many people in Mississippi who will go to any length, even violence, to prevent that [integrated schools, voting rights], I am afraid, I am doing what I can. I can see the possible time when I shall have to leave my native state, something as the Jew had to flee from Germany during Hitler." On 6 September issues dispatch from Rome on murder of Emmett Till, a young Negro from Chicago killed while in Mississippi: "Because if we in America have reached that point in our desperate culture when we must murder children, no matter for what reason or what color, we don't deserve to survive, and probably won't." Publishes *Big Woods* with Random House, 14 October; includes parts of "A Justice" and "Delta Autumn." Addresses Southern Historical Association in Peabody Hotel, Memphis, on 10 November (talk published in *Three Views of the Segregation Decision* by Southern Regional Council in 1956).
1956	In February interview with Russell Warren Howe, is said to have remarked that he would "fight for Mississippi against the United States, even if it meant going out into the street and shooting Negroes." Remark published by London *Sunday*

Times, 4 March; by *The Reporter* magazine (New York), 22 March; repeated in *Time* magazine and denied by Faulkner, 19 April. On 5 March publishes "A Letter to the North" in *Life* magazine, pleading that the North should "go slow now" and allow the South to resolve its own internal racial conflict. On 16 April at age 88, W. E. B. DuBois, a founder of National Association for the Advancement of Colored People, challenges Faulkner to debate on integration at courthouse in Sumner, Mississippi, site of trial for the murder of Emmett Till. Faulkner wires DuBois 18 April: "I DO NOT BELIEVE THERE IS A DEBATABLE POINT BETWEEN US. WE BOTH AGREE IN ADVANCE THAT THE POSITION YOU WILL TAKE IS RIGHT MORALLY LEGALLY AND ETHICALLY. IF IT IS NOT EVIDENT TO YOU THAT THE POSITION I TAKE IN ASKING FOR MODERATION AND PATIENCE IS RIGHT PRACTICALLY THEN WE WILL BOTH WASTE OUR BREATH IN DEBATE." In June publishes "On Fear: the South in Labor" (on racial issues) in *Harper's.* Sends Ober "Letter to the Leaders of the Negro Race" on 27 June at request of *Ebony* magazine (where it is published in September) as response to remarks he made in Howe interview (see Appendix III). Faulkner's biographer Joseph Blotner later comments, "This essay would serve only to affirm this label [gradualist] in the minds of white liberals and to discredit him with Negro activists" (1974; 1609–10). *Requiem for a Nun,* adapted as a play by Camus, opens in Paris, 20 September.

1957   Receives Silver Medal of Athens Academy on 28 March, "as one chosen by the Greek Academy to represent the principle that man shall be free." Publishes *The Town* with Random House, 1 May. Writes another letter to Memphis *Commercial Appeal* against school segregation, 15 September.

1958   On 29 January president of University of Virginia, where Faulkner is visiting writer, refuses to appoint him to permanent position (partly, it is thought, because of Faulkner's views on segregation). "A Word to Virginians," a class session on race at the university, is recorded live on 20 February.

1959   Broadway production of *Requiem for a Nun,* adapted from both Faulkner and Camus, premieres 28 January. Publishes *The Mansion* with Random House, 13 November.

1961   On 3 April, in press conference in Caracas, Venezuela, during trip for U.S. State Department, answers questions about racial issue in America, assigning different responsibilities to each race in search of solution. On 11 June, *New York Times* announces

Chronology

William Faulkner Foundation (begun by Faulkner); half its purpose is to promote education of blacks in Mississippi.

1962 In New York on 24 May, Eudora Welty presents Faulkner with Gold Medal for Fiction on behalf of American Academy of Arts and Letters. Publishes *The Reivers* with Random House, 4 June. On 6 July dies suddenly of a heart attack at 1:30 a.m. in a private clinic in Byhalia, Mississippi, 45 miles from Oxford.

1973 On 22 August, *Flags in the Dust* finally published, as he had wished in 1927, by Random House, in an edition by Douglas Day.

LITERARY AND
HISTORICAL CONTEXT

1

Background

When *Go Down, Moses and Other Stories* was first published in 1942, Faulkner was mildly shocked. The work, he insisted, was a novel, not a collection of stories, and the title was to be changed back to the way he first had it; *and Other Stories* was removed from the title of every subsequent edition of the work. As always, he knew what he was talking about and what he meant to do. The chapters, like those of other novels of the early 1940s, might have separate titles, but they are tightly integrated—by theme, plot, character, metaphor—in countless ways that made them intimately related and separated only at significant cost to their meaning and effect.

In this book, even though we will forcefully deconstruct the novel into episodes for study, we will do so only to demonstrate even more clearly how tightly the whole work is woven together. For the apparent figure in the carpet—the saga of the McCaslin family—is only the surface technique Faulkner uses to study the sociological, psychological, and economic forces of Southern history that are at once its claims to grandeur and to defeat. The result is arguably Faulkner's most comprehensive and enduring portrait of Yoknapatawpha and of the South—a work of amazing insight, of unmatched power, and of haunting beauty. At the same time, *Go Down, Moses* discloses those ideas and truths that Faulkner had spent much of his career avoiding, for the most part, until he wrote this novel.

This is not the first impression *Go Down, Moses* generally makes on its readers. They tend to read "Was" as a tall tale, "The Fire and the Hearth" as a story about confidence men, "Pantaloon in Black" as a story of racial hatred, and the hunting trilogy—"The Old People," "The Bear," and "Delta Autumn"—as the bildungsroman of young Ike McCaslin growing up in idyllic woods, who finds the woods disappearing with his maturity and destroyed in his old age. The final story, "Go Down, Moses," is often seen as a kind of coda about the present.

The false chronology of that presentation—although it is, deliberately, the order of the chapters in the novel—is misleading, or at least deliberately obscurantic, as we shall soon see. But even if we attempt to describe what happens in each chapter, rather than categorize it in subgenres of fiction that have been worn down into classifications and clichés over time, we shall at once have a general picture that is quite different and one that will begin to be more reliable.

Let us look at the novel's chapters again, then: "Was" tells the story of two middle-aged white men who attempt, with mixed success, to exercise control and order over the blacks on their plantation and the neighbors next to it. "The Fire and the Hearth" examines, in the present, the elderly blacks who were freed in their youth as a result of the Civil War. "The Old People," "The Bear," and "Delta Autumn" portray the descendants of the white plantation owners in "Was," who find they must struggle even harder with the freed blacks at the same time that they must struggle harder with their own ancestry and inheritance. The idyllic days of youthful hunts in the woods have been ended by the lumber industry and the incursion of the railroad, showing that the domination of nature is no more secure than the domination of slaves over time; both are exploitative, dissatisfying, and impermanent. Any attempt to deny change, moreover, leads to death (with Sam Fathers), to total compromise (with Cass Edmonds) or relinquishment (with Ike McCaslin), or to madness (with Boon Hogganbeck). That the blacks of the novel's present fare little better than their Indian or white counterparts is shown by the fates of Rider in "Pantaloon in Black" and Butch Beauchamp in "Go Down, Moses"—who, for all their differences, come to ends strangely yet tellingly similar.

Looked at this way, each episode is related to the others in tracing the effects of plantation life and slave economy, while each chapter breaks from the others to examine those effects from a different perspective. Together, however, they consistently build a realistic picture of Southern life during the plantation era and beyond—through the War Between the States, Reconstruction, the advent of industrialization and mercantilism, and the earliest signs of a movement toward civil rights.

This portrait is no accident, and in many ways it is an act of deliberate compensation, if not defiance. Faulkner wrote *Absalom, Absalom!* in part under the shadow of his great-grandfather, Colonel William C. Falkner, a best-selling author of hoopskirt romance and a slaveowner from northern Ripley, Mississippi. Now he would write *Go Down, Moses* in an attempt to free himself, and Southern fiction, from such nostalgic make-believe. He would also write a new kind of plantation novel that would free fiction from the more serious but no less romantic works of such Southern novelists as Ellen Glasgow, Andrew Lytle, and Caroline Gordon.

These writers took part in a long tradition of plantation fiction perpetuating a legend of antebellum civilization centered on dashing cavaliers, beautiful Southern belles, and nobel plantation owners toward whom blacks remained loving and loyal retainers. John Pendleton Kennedy's *Swallow Barn* (1832) is generally credited with beginning the tradition; this portrait of a Virginia plantation during the seventeenth century presents the planter's house as a center of morality, good manners, and graceful simplicity—the sort of life Sophonsiba wishes for Warwick. After the war the tradition was more double-edged: plantation pride was subtly countered by the threat of family loss and dissolution, while the plantation system itself suggested a kind of tragic Eden. If Thomas Nelson Page's *Ole Virginia* (1887) depicted the pleasures of master-slave relations, Joel Chandler Harris's *Uncle Remus: His Songs and Sayings* (1880), based on authentic black trickster tales, showed—whether it meant to or not—the ways in which blacks could rebel against the social system. In later fiction Harris stressed the slave themes even more. The title story of *Free Joe and Other Georgian Sketches* (1887) examines the life of a freed black man in the world of slavery; in *Balaam and His Master* (1881) the story "Where's Duncan" looks at the effects of miscegenation on a white master who fathers a black son. The morality of slavery and the fate of blacks after the war is more openly confronted in *The Grandissimes* (1880) by George Washington Cable, where the platitudes of the northern-born Joseph Frowenfeld and the experiences of Honoré Grandissime begin to raise the same racial issues that fuel the commissary scene of "The Bear," while Honoré's half-brother, an "f.m.c." or "free man of color," loves a quadroon woman who in turn loves the white Honoré, raising many of the problems of miscegenation that Ike and others wrestle with in *Go Down, Moses*. Moreover, the whole Grandissime clan is obsessed with its own slave history, much as the McCaslins are obsessed with the Beauchamps, although the Grandissime slave, Bras-Coupé, is a noble African prince who cannot endure bondage and thus seems a distant ancestor of Rider. There is no evidence that Faulkner knew or used any of these novels of plantation life and family romance, but the tradition, long established, was one he knew in general terms. Faulkner's *Go Down, Moses* was to contrast sharply with that tradition, telling Southern history the way it was, in order to measure more clearly and more securely the conditions in which he and other Southerners found themselves in 1940. To understand just what new resources Faulkner would draw on to break from the fictional traditions with which he grew up, we will look first at the history of plantations and of the attendant slavery, with special focus on northern Mississippi, where the mythical Yoknapatawpha County is situated. Then we will look at other resources on which he drew, especially the experiences of his own family, in chapter 2 of this study, "Foreground." Finally, in chapter 3, "Other Grounds," we shall see how his revolutionary rewriting of plantation fiction fared with some of his earliest and most important critics.

MISSISSIPPI PLANTATIONS: A BRIEF HISTORY

For a half-century following the Revolutionary War, much of northern Mississippi was Indian territory, despite increasing interest in land by the federal government. But in 1830 the Choctaws gave in to persuasion and signed over their claims to northern and central Mississippi in return for new land in Oklahoma and a cash settlement in the Treaty of Dancing Rabbit Creek. Then, in 1832, the Chickasaws, a more warlike tribe, did likewise in the Treaty of Pontotoc (see chronology).

Immediately, white settlers began flooding in, purchasing large tracts of largely virgin land at low cost. While some of these new arrivals were crude frontiersmen, like Thomas Sutpen, others were descendants of wealthy plantation owners in Virginia, the Carolinas, and, more recently, Alabama and Tennessee, and many of them brought dozens or hundreds of slaves with them, as L. Q. C. McCaslin did. Their plan was to raise cotton: the rapidly increasing textile mills in New England and burgeoning markets in England and elsewhere in Europe were clamoring for it, and the vast expanses of land, along with the high prices cotton consistently got, made raising that crop an irresistible temptation. The prices that cotton could fetch, in fact, rose through the 1830s, bringing a panic and a short-term depression in 1837. But recovery came early, and the 1840s and 1850s were also boom years for the new South. By 1860 the glowing future caused an ebullient clerk of court for Lafayette County (on which Faulkner would largely model his own Yoknapatawpha County) to write in his office in Oxford, the county seat, "good Times in our County. Cotton worth 10 3/4 Corn one dollar per bushel Bacon 15 cents per lb. Negroe men 1500 to 2000-hundred dollars and woman from 1300 to 1800 and times Still looking up So press up Boys."[2]

In good times or poor, the settlers were buoyed by a philosophy that farming was God's work. As one New Hampshire pastor told his farming congregation, "The fields we cultivate are an emblem of the moral field of the world. The labor we bestow upon them is a striking representation of that moral and religious culture which should be given to individuals and society."[3] Orators and agricultural societies in the northern and southern states alike saw working the land by whatever means—including the means of slavery—as God's work, and the farmers themselves as God's keepers of the land, perpetuators and symbols of God's trust. Just how deeply imbedded such a religion of the land was in the people can be seen in the readiness with which Ike McCaslin turns to sacred doctrine in addressing the history of the McCaslin plantation in *Go Down, Moses*. It did not take long for the frontier spirit and the entrepreneurial motivations both to be lost in this sense of a mission that allied God's will with man's own.[4]

Go Down, Moses is Faulkner's primary work concerning plantation life and economy: its founding, its operations, and its consequences. That he would need to address these themes sooner or later in his fiction was unavoidable, as plantations were the focus and basis for antebellum Southern society and much of its fictional tradition (as illustrated by the Scotch-Irish Fincastles in Ellen Glasgow's *Vein of Iron*). In that era, Southern society was pyramidal. At the top were plantation owners with large slaveholdings (usually calculated as 50 or more), who managed the land, established the economy, and kept control by amassing and retaining a vast majority of the wealth and power. (By the 1860s the slaveholding elite of Mississippi numbered 10,000 families owning roughly 50,000 blacks.) But in the caste system of that society, the enslaved blacks had their counterparts among whites of considerably less wealth and power than the plantation owners: the yeoman farmers, who might themselves own one or two slaves but who often worked alongside them, and the poor whites, despised by whites and blacks alike, who often unsuccessfully tried to scrabble out a living in the harder clay soil of northern Mississippi and whose indolence in some cases could make them almost totally dependent on the kindness of others. The prevailing class system, imported in large measure from Europe through other Southern states, was more or less immutable, so that education was largely limited to the wealthy, and the pyramid remained fixed and unthreatened.

The landed (if homegrown in some part) aristocracy were, first and last, tough-minded businessmen, keen capitalists with an eye on investment and both eyes on profit. Numerous books and journals published for plantation owners stressed accounting and accountability; one of them (which sounds like one L. Q. C. McCaslin might have read) urges that

> The overseer shall keep a plantation book, in which he shall register the birth and name of each negro that is born; the name of each negro that died, and specify the disease that killed him. He shall also keep in it the weights of the daily picking of each hand,

the mark, number and weight of each bale of cotton, and the time
of sending the same to market; and all other occurrences, relating
to the crop, the weather, and all other matters pertaining to the
plantation that he may deem advisable.[5]

As markets increased, manuals for plantation management were in
much greater supply than the advice given by someone like Jonathan
Edwards the younger, who told the Connecticut Abolition Society in
1792 that slaveholders would in time need to "[raise] their [slaves']
color to a partial whitness" through miscegenation or else, in time, will
to them all their lands (Sundquist, 146). If antebellum northern
Mississippi heard any sentiments of abolition, they appear to have
been drowned out by increasing economic fortune and the dominant
belief in the sacred mission to cultivate God's earth.

The Civil War (which the South saw as the War of Northern
Invasion) freed the slaves legally in 1863 and brought down the basis of
the South's whole financial enterprise. While some wealthy landowners
managed to retain some of their fortune, it was vastly reduced; still
known locally as aristocracy or "quality," they depended more on reputation and the past than conditions of the present. The defeat of the
Confederate States of America, in fact, is still bitter in part because it
now seems excessive, borne not only by those who fought the Union
army but in turn by their children and even their grandchildren. Mili-
tary defeat meant economic and political defeat. Joel Williamson has
noted that "Over the two generations after Appomattox, the South
became imperial America's first colony. The reduction was effected by
discriminatory tariffs and railroad freight charges, by high interest rates
and low wages, and by holding the South to the production of low-
priced raw materials and the consumption of relatively costly finished
goods produced in the North" (1993, 13).

Large shareholdings after 1865 were often preserved by dividing
them into smaller parcels for tenant farmers and sharecroppers (as *Go
Down, Moses* illustrates with the tenant farm Lucas Beauchamp owns).
By the 1930s the Works Progress Administration guide to Mississippi
notes that the state has 225,617 tenant families, both white and black,
constituting three classes. Renters hired land for fixed annual amounts in

cash or crops. Sharetenants supplied their own equipment and animals and earned a fixed percentage of the cash crop (cotton) in return for working the land. Sharecroppers paid in labor only for use of the land and were given implements, animals, seed, fertilizer, home, fuel, and food. Renters were few; sharecroppers were largest in number (it is the sharecropper's position George Wilkins hopes to inherit in chapter 2 of *Go Down, Moses* by marrying Nat Beauchamp). Sharecroppers composed 135,293 of the 225,617 tenant families in Mississippi in 1930. And their terms for livelihood were not especially favorable. A typical contract stipulated that "You the tenant further agrees that if you violate this contract, or neglects, or abandons or fails or (in Mr. ———'s judgment) violates this contract or fails to properly work or till the land early or at proper times, or in case you should become disabled or legally sick or hurt while working this land or should die during the term of your lease, or fails to gather or save the crops when made, or fails to pay the rents or advances made by me, whenever due,"[6] then the contract would be canceled at the owner's option, all debts would immediately be due, and the land would be sold or assigned to another party. Dependency and submission were thus not only economic terms but also, in many ways, habits of mind that extended the practices of slavery instituted before the war.

BLACK LIFE ON THE PLANTATION

What initially distinguished northern Mississippi from the northern United States, then, was that "White people owned black people, and from that single fact flowed a whole broad stream that permeated life in Mississippi and made it qualitatively different from that in the nonslaveholding states" (Williamson 1993, 29). More than half of the people of Mississippi were slaves in the 1850s (435,000, or 57 percent), and while black families were kept together to prevent their discontent, black men had no economic leverage, making their families matriarchal, the women having more importance as breeders of future generations of slaves. The effects of this "peculiar institution" were everywhere: in the stores and goods sold, in churches and religions practiced, in homes, in courtrooms, in prisons, in government offices, in state militia. The white men who operated these segments of Southern society were thus daily implicated in slavery as well (and often dependent on it); the local "patrols" that ranged the streets of towns like Oxford to keep people in their place were telling symbols of the Southern way of life. Even after the war, deliberate impoverishment coupled with deliberate lack of education, kept society stable by keeping blacks in their place and ensured those virtues—humility, servility, dependence, patience—that were required of them. Mississippi, in fact, was the first southern state to enact the Black Codes following the war; these laws forbade blacks to vote, to keep firearms, or to "make insulting gestures," and they provided that any black 18 years or older who was unemployed might be considered a vagrant, fined 50 dollars, and turned over to any "master or mistress." Such perspectives were fostered—at times with the best of intentions by an Uncle Buck or Uncle Buddy, as in chapter 1 of *Go Down, Moses*—as a form of protective paternalism. As one southern planter put it in 1853,

> The fundamental principles upon which the system is based, are simply these: that all living on the plantation, whether colored or not, are members of the same family, and to be treated as such— that they all have their respective duties to perform, and that the happiness and prosperity of all will be in proportion to the fidelity with which each member discharges his part. I take occasion to inculcate repeatedly that, as the patriarch (not tyrant) of the family, my laws when clearly promulgated, must be obeyed—that, as patriarch, it is my duty to protect their rights, to feed, clothe and house them properly—to attend to them carefully when sick—to provide for all their proper wants—to promote peace, harmony and good feeling, and so far as practicable, their individual comfort. On the other hand, the servants are distinctly informed that they have to work and obey my laws, or suffer the penalty.[7]

This paternal metaphor was always in active play—and the use of black wet nurses for white babies and black playmates for white children encouraged such a sense of family.

Another natural outgrowth of slavery was miscegenation. The extent of white-black sexual relations is impossible now to measure.

From 1860 on applying the notion that one drop of black blood made a person black or mulatto (it was never reciprocal; a drop of white blood never made a person white), federal census statistics attempted to record the distinction; they indicate that mulattoes made up 8.5 percent (or 37,200) of Mississippi's black population in 1860 and 11.5 percent (or 85,166) of it in 1890. But such criteria for inclusion in the finely calibrated categories of black vs. mulatto were often difficult to judge and were not always openly admitted. In the early years of the nineteenth century, miscegenation on plantations was not uncommon. Even during Reconstruction—in the state constitution of 1869—Mississippi recognized common-law unions; in 1870 the ban on inter-marriage was repealed. But only a small number of interracial marriages took place, and they were often ridiculed. In 1876 such unions were again prohibited, and an injunction against them was made part of the new state constitution in 1890.

But legal marriage is one thing; relations are another. If white opposition to interracial unions was nearly unanimous, sexual congress between white men and black women was widely tolerated in practice. (Sexual congress between black men and white women, however, was not acceptable at all and was frequently the grounds for lynching black men.) From antebellum days onward, many white men conceived black "shadow families," which they cared for as conscientiously as their own more public white families. Before the war, white planters might send their black relations northward to freedom through manu-mission and a new start in life; before and after the war, they often made mulatto children beneficiaries in their wills, as L. Q. C. McCaslin and his sons do. But during the war and after, such liaisons were often embarrassing, as the Confederates battled to keep the peculiar institu-tion alive and tensions over race, North and South, escalated. It was no less embarrassing, of course, for the white planter's white wife. Mary Chesnut confronts this frankly in her diary: "His wife and daughters, in their purity and innocence, are supposed never to dream of what is as plain before their eyes as the sunlight," she remarks. Elsewhere, referring to Harriet Beecher Stowe's *Uncle Tom's Cabin,* she writes, "You see, Mrs. Stowe did not hit the sorest spot. She makes Legree a bachelor" (quoted in William Taylor, 169).

In a society where boundaries thus became blurred and permissiveness was an unspoken fact of life, other means were taken to keep blacks in line and white authority paramount. Whippings seem to have been frequent, sometimes caused only by suspicion or the desire to intimidate, as Allison Davis found in field interviews of Mississippi landlords and tenants in two Mississippi counties between 1932 and 1935.[8] Lynching was also made deliberately public and monstrous because it was meant to be deliberately admonitory and repressive (for local cases of which Faulkner knew, see Appendix II). In 1939 anthropologist Hortense Powdermaker writes, in *After Freedom*, that by the age of puberty, white people know "that the Negro is cut out to be a victim, that the Negro cannot exact justice if he is wronged and dare not wreak revenge for himself." She adds that "[t]he attitude of the whites and of the courts which they control is one of complaisance toward violence among the Negroes, and even toward intra-Negro homicide." There were thus two standards of justice: "When a white man kills a Negro, it is hardly considered murder. When a Negro kills a white man, conviction is ensured, provided the case is not settled immediately by lynch law."[9] The contemporary historian James W. Siver, Faulkner's friend, describes "[a] classic example of lynching as a means of social control" in 1928—a story of a chase (with 3,000 cars and 6,000 whites) ending in an act of savage murder and gratuitous mutilation (85–86). But by then, the statistics on lynchings in Mississippi showed that they were on the decline: there had been 57 in the 1910s, in contrast to 28 in the 1920s. Fifteen or fewer lynchings occurred in the 1930s, and the last official traditional lynching in the state was recorded in 1935. These grim statistics are the necessary framework for chapters 3 and 7 of *Go Down, Moses*.

BLACK SURVIVAL

Blacks survived in such an atmosphere of intimidation and fear by means of several strategies. Perhaps most fundamental was what W. E. B. DuBois referred to as "double-consciousness"—"a sense of always looking at one's self through the eyes of others, of measuring one's soul by the tape of a world that looks on in amused contempt and pity."[10]

One strategy was to adopt ideas of the dominant white culture. For instance, blacks developed their own caste system, based on the division of labor among slaves or servants who worked and lived in the house of the white landlords, who were seen superior to field hands, who lived in the quarters designated for blacks (and both were considered superior to "poor white trash"; one black chant goes, "My name's Sam, I don't give a damn; I'd rather be a nigger than a poor white man"). Religion offered another means of survival. Although blacks took on the Christianity of whites, they developed their own form of gospel service and gospel music, which records their needs and reactions. On a recent trip to the South, V. S. Naipaul noted, "The songs seemed to be variations on a single line. 'What would I do without Jesus?'"[11] But in fact they took many perspectives: passive resistance ("We'll Outlast the Storm"); a better life to come ("Deep River"); the cry for a redeemer now ("Go Down, Moses").

Blacks' reactions to their social condition took various forms as well. Bertram Wyatt-Brown has summarized them as three "major types of servility. . . . The first is . . . ritualized compliance in which self-regard is retained. The second is the socialization of subordination, a natural acceptance of circumstance that involves the incorporation of shame. The third type of subordination is the adoption of 'samboism,' as it may be called, or shamelessness. None of the forms of subservience is exclusive, for each merges into another with as much variation and contradictoriness as might be found in any individual" (quoted in Harris, 133). But the role-playing that such reactions employ can lead to self-deprecation, self-hatred, or growing rage, as Lucas and Rider demonstrate in *Go Down, Moses*.

Such accommodating behavior can be shrewd, duplicitous, or mocking. Robert R. Moton, the head of the Tuskegee Institute, said in 1929, "Much of what is regarded as racially characteristic of the Negro is nothing more than his artful and adroit accommodation of his manners and methods to what he knows to be the weakness and foibles of his white neighbors. Knowing what is expected of him, and knowing too what he himself wants, the Negro craftily uses his knowledge to anticipate opposition and to eliminate friction in securing his desires" (quoted in Peavy, 40).

Background

Many, such as Mary Chesnut of South Carolina, could be taken in: "We had a wonderful scene here last Sunday—an old African—who heard he was free & did not at his helpless old age relish the idea. So he wept & prayed, kissed hands, rolled over on the floor until the boards of the piazza were drenched with his tears. He seemed to worship his master & evidently regarded the white race as some superior order of beings, he prostrated himself so humbly"[12] (an outrageously obvious enactment of samboism). In *Go Down, Moses,* Lucas is quick to practice such samboism, especially in "The Fire and the Hearth." But the practice is often much more complicated, as the black poet Paul Laurence Dunbar reveals in "We Wear the Mask":

> We wear the mask that grins and lies,
> It hides our cheeks and shades our eyes,—
> This debt we pay to human guile;
> With torn and bleeding hearts we smile,
> And mouth with myriad subtleties.
> Why should the world be overwise,
> In counting all our tears and sighs?
> Nay, let them only see us, while
> We wear the mask.
>
> We smile, but, O great Christ, our cries
> To thee from tortured souls arise.
> We sing, but oh the clay is vile
> Beneath our feet, and long the mile;
> But let the world dream otherwise,
> We wear the mask!

In "The Fire and the Hearth," Roth is always aware of Lucas's techniques, although his reaction is made more difficult because Lucas is married to his black mammy, Molly, whom he deeply loves. In "Go Down, Moses," Gavin Stevens seems oblivious to both the samboism that enraged Butch Beauchamp and the samboism so stoutly denied by Molly, her brother, and Miss Worsham, the white woman with whom Molly grew up. For someone as outspoken as they—or someone like Faulkner's contemporary in Mississippi, black novelist Richard Wright—such demeaning behavior is intolerable. In his autobiography,

Black Boy, Wright recalls how a black elevator operator named Shorty played the clown to a Memphis white man, offering to be kicked for a quarter. The enraged Wright scolded him to no avail. "'Listen, nigger,' he said to me, 'my ass is tough and quarters is scarce.'"[13]

This complicated and often subtle range of felt need, behavior, and self-judgment among both whites and blacks is the essential fabric of *Go Down, Moses,*[14] the cultural conditioning from which Faulkner weaves the entire novel. If we place these facts alongside a more romantic plantation novel like *Barren Ground* by Ellen Glasgow or the novels of Caroline Gordon; alongside a hunting novel like Gordon's *Aleck Maury Sportsman;* or against the starkly racist portraits of freed blacks in the works of Thomas Dixon—*The Leopard's Spots* is the most notorious—we can see how distant these works of fiction are as predecessors of Faulkner's *Go Down, Moses.* They are totally unlike the novel we are about to read. On the other hand, if we keep referring back to these facts in reading *Go Down, Moses,* we will see how Faulkner broke from the tradition of Southern plantation fiction and how, in that departure, he was able to craft a novel far more powerful because it makes vivid so much of the Southern history that informed the northern Mississippi he knew best.

2

Foreground

William Faulkner's family never owned a plantation; the first Falkner in his line to settle in Mississippi (around 1841) was entrepreneurial enough—investing in land, writing books, founding a railroad, and leading his own regiment in the first major battle of Confederate forces. Yet no one, Frederick R. Karl says of Faulkner, "could have been more the product of his time and place. Faulkner's every fiber was shaped by his birth in the Deep South, a Mississippi birth" in 1897 (4). Indeed, on every page of *Go Down, Moses*, "primarily the story of what it means to be a descendant and an inheritor," as David Minter puts it (187), Faulkner displays his own Southern legacies.

As a child, Faulkner learned intimately the Tallahatchie River bottom in northern Lafayette County, where he hunted with his father, Murry; the site of Major DeSpain's camp in "The Bear" is in the approximate location on the map of Yoknapatawpha County which Faulkner drew for *Absalom, Absalom!* (1936) as the Cain plantation which was one of Murry Falkner's favorite hunting grounds. That land, poorly drained and heavily forested, harbored bears and even wolves as late as 1920 (when Faulkner was 23). Later, in his adult years, Faulkner went on annual hunting parties based at the camp of

The Washington Price house, a possible model for the McCaslin mansion. *Photograph by Arthur F. Kinney.*

"General" James Stone, the father of his boyhood friend Phil Stone, some thirty miles west of Oxford in Panola County, at the edge of the Tallahatchie and Yazoo Delta. Stone's lodge was reached by going from Oxford west to Batesville and then taking a logging train built in 1910 southwestward into the Big Woods. That train resembles the one that Ike and Boon take (back to Batesville, in effect, and then, changing trains, on up to Memphis). After the Stone family sold this land to lumbering interests in the late 1930s, Faulkner and his fellow hunters moved further south into the delta, finding virgin wilderness close to the Big Sunflower River near Anguilla, 150 miles from Oxford.[15] Scenes in "The Old People," "The Bear," and "Delta Autumn" draw directly on his experiences. They also show Faulkner's love of hunting; quick to teach its lessons in turn to his own stepson Malcolm Franklin, whom he took hunting, as he took his nephew Jimmy, Faulkner once punished Malcolm severely for shooting at a bird in the nest, betraying the hunter's code (Wittenberg, 197).[16]

As Faulkner began to earn money writing, he began buying up land—first the antebellum home of Robert Shegog in Oxford; then a 35-acre tract of land abutting it, known locally as Bailey's Woods; and then, in the later 1930s, a 320-acre farm 13 miles east of town (see chronology). Faulkner asked his brother John to manage it at first, but clearly it is the model for the McCaslin plantation, and Faulkner came to know it intimately: on Saturdays he would drive out and work in the commissary, surrounded by the smells of cheese and leather and keeping track of the purchases of his black tenant farmers, both large and small (Blotner 1984, 419). Faulkner's major biographer thinks Faulkner had a fascination with ledgers and with their means of accountability, and even conjectures that he may have seen one in nearby Taylor that had an entry for a Carothers Edmonds (Blotner, 2:1091). Later Faulkner put the black "Uncle" Ned Barnett in charge—and constantly wrangled with him, much as Roth wrangles with Lucas.

OTHER LOCAL RESOURCES

Faulkner drew on other family and friends as well. A famous incident in the life of his great-grandfather William C. Falkner (a popular writer whom Faulkner emulated as a boy) was his duel with Robert Hindman. Hindman attempted to kill Falkner with his pistol, but the gun misfired (Williamson 1993, 20), just as Lucas's gun misfires during his duel with Zack in "The Fire and the Hearth." Faulkner's nephew Jim recalls another story, which may have contributed to "Pantaloon in Black": "Double Dip and Ammonia live in a house out in the back and down the hill from our house, and they have lived on the place and worked for us for years, even before he had to go to Parchman, the state penitentiary, for a few years because [Double Dip] had to kill Dusty in a crap game that time when Dusty tried to pass the smaller part of a torn dollar bill to him."[17] Faulkner may have combined his own recollection of Double Dip with that of Elwood Higginbotham (see Appendix II).

Emily Whitehurst Stone, wife of Phil Stone, has written that Stone Stop, near the Stones' residence before they left the Delta for Oxford, was near land owned by Phil's great-uncles Theophilus and Amodeus Potts, "whom everybody called Buck and Buddy" (see Kinney 1990, 15–16). Lewis M. Dabney has even located a possible source for Boon Hogganbeck. "He is partly drawn from Buster Callicot, the senior Falkner's table foreman, with whom Faulkner told of having bought a Texas pony. . . . John Faulkner says his brother and Buster took the Memphis trip to buy whiskey for Stone's [hunting] camp, and this comic scene [in "The Bear"] is autobiographical in feeling."[18]

Faulkner was still hunting in the late fall of 1940, as he was putting the finishing revisions on *Go Down, Moses*. It was necessary therapy even then. "I spent last week in November in the big woods after deer but never shot my rifle," he wrote Random House. "One nice thing about the woods: off there hunting, I dont fret and stew so much about Europe. But I'm only 43, I'm afraid I'm going to the damn thing [World War II] yet" (Blotner 1974, 2:1065). But he failed here to report the near-tragedy of that trip in the Delta near Anguilla:

> Bob Harkins led them on [Faulkner's] forty-ninth consecutive hunt. "Old Man Bob" Evans, Uncle Bud Miller, and Ike Roberts followed him in the hierarchy of the hunt. Then came the younger men, such as Felix Linder and William Faulkner. Negotiating the last eight miles by motorboat, they would pitch their tents and make camp. At first, they would eat pork, but before a full day passed, old Ad Bush would be cooking squirrel and coon. They would go out in the four-o'clock darkness, making their way through the thick brush into the deep woods, the leashed dogs sniffing and barking. Then the drive would begin, the hunters poised at their stands for the dash of the buck. At the end of the long day they would sit around the campfire drinking

whiskey. . . . Faulkner enjoyed it. . . . He told some of the memorable tales, but most of the time he would listen. . . .

He would drink moderately at first. Then his tempo would speed up. It way have been on this hunt that Ad Bush went to Uncle Bud one morning and told him he ought to go and take a look at Mr. Bill. Miller found him unconscious and ashen. Their alarm mounted because they were afraid he had suffered a kidney seizure of some sort. As they tried to figure out a way to get him out quickly, the sound of a motorboat reached them—"the best sound I ever heard in my life," Red Brite called it. Back in Oxford, Dr. Culley told them a few more hours would have been too late. Alcohol. together with the weeks and months of worry and irritation, had done its work. Brite did not know if it was a perforated ulcer the doctor had feared, but whatever it was, it had been a close call. (Blotner 1984, 424)

This incident, with its feeling of doom and the approach of death, with its surrender of the hunt to feelings of exhaustion, clearly contributed to the conception of "Delta Autumn."

LOCAL HISTORY

Faulkner also shows historical knowledge of his own Lafayette County in *Go Down, Moses*. While he may have taken the name of his fictional county directly from the name of the river near the southern boundary of Lafayette County, he apparently was not content with local legend that *Yoknapatawpha* is an Indian word for "water runs slow through flat land." Rather, he seems to have gone to a 1915 *Dictionary of Choctaw Language*, in which the word is broken down as follows:

ik patafo, a., unplowed.

patafa, pp., split open; plowed, furrowed; tilled.

yakni, n., the earth; . . . soil; ground; nation; . . . district. . . .

yakni patafa, pp., furrowed land; fallowed land.[19]

The literal meaning of *Yoknapatawpha*, then, is "plowed or cultivated land or district," sounding much like what the white settlers would make it into; this is made more pointedly ironic in Faulkner's short story "A Courtship," in which an Indian calls his land *Plantation* (*Collected Stories*, 361). It seems even more certain that Faulkner read about Indian burial rites, because the burial of Sam Fathers in "The Bear" follows in detail the practices described in an article published in 1900, near an account of his own great-grandfather's fiction, in the *Publications of the Mississippi Historical Society* (Dabney, 37); Faulkner simply changed Choctaw rites to Chickasaw.

Any one of a number of settlers of Lafayette County might have served Faulkner as a model for L. Q. C. McCaslin, but the closest was Washington Price, whose large plantation 12 miles east of Oxford, near Tula (it was the largest in the area), and whose extensive slaveholdings (he is thought to have arrived in Mississippi with 200 slaves) made him legendary in the region, then as now. Price was born in October 1803 in Wake County, North Carolina, to Thomas and Rebekah Robertson Price, themselves the owners of a large plantation near Raleigh, which he inherited. He first moved to the area of Jackson, Tennessee, where he married Frances Bushrod Harris in 1836; in 1837 the couple moved to Lafayette County and built their home, Oak Grove, in a stand of oak trees high above the Yocona River. It is a unique home (still standing, it has been moved to the area known as Denmark and renamed "7Cs") with a two-story portico that seems rather boldly to enlarge a some-what smaller and lower house with the usual two symmetrical wings off the central hallway. (Lucas's description of Carothers's house [44] fits this home almost exactly.) Price's operation is summarized in the 1850 census records, now housed in the Department of Archives and History at Jackson, Mississippi: at that time he had 5,000 acres of land, valued at $6,000, and farm implements worth $4,000; his plantation annually produced 4,000 bushels of corn and 115 bales of cotton. Today, according to Jack Case Wilson, "More than any other house in Lafayette County, the old home of Washington Price retains the appearance and feel of an 1840s Mississippi plantation."[20]

According to local legend, early generations of the Price family made cash gifts (not recorded in their wills submitted to probate) to a black family named Boles, thought possibly to be related to them. One living member of the Boles family recalls that either Washington or Bem Price had a daughter named Margaret by one of the slaves on the old Price plantation. Taking the name of Boles from a white family that farmed part of the Price land, Margaret went to work in a rooming house in nearby Holly Springs, where at the age of 15 she met and fell in love with a white man from Oxford. The two were privately married and raised a number of children; one of their sons, Robert Boles, Sr., founded a shoe repair shop on the Oxford town square, which Faulkner regularly patronized.

Molly Beauchamp seems likely to have been drawn not from a member of the Boles family but from Faulkner's own mammy, Caroline Barr, who died just as he was completing *Go Down, Moses*; the novel is dedicated to her. She was small and frail, like Molly, and had Molly's iron determination. Moreover, as James Early reports, "Molly's numerous skirts and underskirts seem to have been suggested by Callie's" (8). Mammy Callie died of a stroke as Faulkner was writing the last chapter of the novel, and he insisted that her funeral be held in the parlor of his home (as Molly wants Butch buried in his hometown). Faulkner requested a chorus drawn from Oxford's three black churches; they stood around the casket singing, among other gospel songs, "Swing Low, Sweet Chariot," and Faulkner "spoke feelingly of her life of devotion and service"[21]—bringing to mind Gavin Stevens's wishes to be involved in Butch's funeral, although he has neither Faulkner's authority nor will in making arrangements.

Faulkner's Understanding of Blacks

Go Down, Moses has more black characters and more major events involving black-white relations than any other of Faulkner's novels. They are varied and often subtle; but his concern also seems obsessive. In Faulkner's South, blacks were a constant presence never fully known to whites. As late as 1942, he dictated the terms of Callie Barr's funeral, rather than allowing her own family to plan it, so as to ensure himself of an occasion for his own deeply felt tribute. While Faulkner was aware of blacks in his society—often uncomfortably so—he was also conditioned by the Mississippi culture in which he was reared.

In 1925, at the time Faulkner began writing, F. P. Gaines wrote that "the popular conception thinks of race relations . . . as always happy"; his own black taxonomy was threefold: the "uncle," the "mammy," and the buffoonish Jim Crow. Simultaneously, a book on the "history of blacks in American films" appeared, entitled *Toms, Coons, Mulattoes, Mammies, and Bucks.* Faulkner's first treatments of blacks in fiction were—however detailed—fundamentally as limited. Primitive black church service seems consoling to two white men at the close of Faulkner's first novel, *Soldiers' Pay,* when they find that their race permits no similar form of release of sorrow.

In his first Yoknapatawpha novel, *Flags in the Dust,* Faulkner introduces his first mulatto, Elnora, born of Colonel Sartoris and a black slave, simple and obedient, who is married to a foolish but manipulative man and mothers a lazy and braggart son. Any attempt by the reader to see these characters as individuals is severely constrained when, later in the novel, Faulkner makes an analogy between blacks and mules, who share the common features of indolence, resentment, and patience while waiting for revenge (Vintage 1974, 314). Even in *The Sound and the Fury,* which Faulkner thought of as his personal and private novel, Deacon is treated as an Uncle Tom, and the intellectual Quentin Compson thinks of blacks as simplistic inversions of whites (Vintage 1990, 82, 86); in part 4, the Reverend Shegog acts like a monkey and speaks in slurred black dialect at the Easter service in Nigger Hollow (a dialect Faulkner attempts to imitate but could not have known first-hand), while Dilsey, the the Compsons' loyal retainer, is portrayed as a faithful mammy whose chief virtue is her consent to serve and protect her white family.

All of these portraits are distant and more or less one-dimensional. Even "Dry September," Faulkner's moving study of a small-town lynching published in 1931, uses the generalized if sympathetic portrait of the black Willie Mays to explore the frustration of empty white lives in Jefferson. This culture-bound understanding of race is stated more openly in a letter Faulkner wrote to the Memphis *Commercial Appeal* in early February 1931. The letter was published on Sunday, February

15, under the caption "Mob Sometimes Right" and, using many of the white racist myths and shibboleths of the time, defends lynching under certain circumstances: "he who was victim of our blundering, also blundered. I have yet to hear," Faulkner writes, "outside of a novel or a story, of a man of any color and with a record beyond reproach, suffering violence at the hands of men who knew him" (quoted McMillen-Polk, 4). "It is the black man's misfortune that he suffers it, just as it is his misfortune that he suffers the following instances of white folks' sentimentality." He then goes on to cite both the stereotype of the manipulative black man—"the colored man [who] had never had title to the land [he claimed] at all, having used, as they do, two or even three separate names in making trades or borrowing money from the government loan associations, and so having used the land tax-free for a year and made a crop and moved on"—and the typically lazy black man such as the one who "went to Detroit years ago, where, he writes back, 'he has not done a lick of work in 15 years, because the white folks up there give him food'" (5). The letter concludes:

> I hold no brief for lynching. No balanced man will deny that mob violence serves nothing, just as he will not deny that a lot of our natural and logical jurisprudence serves nothing either. It just happens that we—mobber and mobbee—live in this age. We will muddle through, and die in our beds, the deserving and the fortunate among us. Of course, with the population what it is, there are some of us that won't. Some will die rich, and some will die on cross-ties soaked with gasoline, to make a holiday. But there is one curious thing about mobs. Like our juries, they have a way of being right. (6)

This forceful letter, with its "baldness of racial attitudes" (3) and "its exculpatory tone and its conventional, myth-ridden white assumptions" (7), is a response to a short letter of gratitude by a black writer commending the attempts of a new organization of Mississippi white women "to eradicate or fight the evils of lynching" (3). While Faulkner may have deliberately exaggerated racist attitudes in order to expose them, Neil R. McMillen and Noel Polk find that the strong abruptness of Faulkner's reply "stands . . . completely in accord with contemporary racial attitudes in white Mississippi and the South generally" (6), noting that 304 lynchings are recorded in Mississippi between the year of Faulkner's birth (1898) and 1931: "he lived and wrote within the very buckle on the great Southern lynching belt—the state with the most total lynchings, the most multiple lynchings, the most per capita, the most female victims, the most victims taken from police custody, the most lynchings without arrest or conviction of mob leaders, the most public support for vigilantism" (7–8).

At the time of this letter, Faulkner had just suffered the inexplicable death of his infant daughter; it has been suggested that he was not totally sober at the time of its composition. But 1931 was a turning point in his writing. Apparently haunted by an actual lynching in his own town—that of Nelse Patton—he set about to write, fictively, a detailed analysis of racial attitudes and lynching in *Light in August*, both deepening and mystifying racial matters by using as a protagonist Joe Christmas, a man who may or may not be partly black. Once embarked on matters of race, he continued with the mulatto Charles Bon in *Absalom, Absalom!*, apparently a mulatto who passes for white in a decade of American novels about passing (Nell Larson's *Passing* is still the best and most authoritative of this subgenre). Faulkner concentrates especially on the fact and fear of miscegenation among the white Sutpens, Coldfields, and Compsons. Indeed, *Go Down, Moses* is arguably the sequel to *Absalom, Absalom!* in that it attempts to examine both the causes and consequences of miscegenation. In both of these novels, black-white relations, and especially the threat of interbreeding, take on a particularly striking force.

FAULKNER'S ANCESTRY AND MISCEGENATION

Joel Williamson has recently suggested why Faulkner became so interested in miscegenation. His great-grandfather whom he emulated, Colonel William Clark Falkner, the "old colonel" of the Falkner family, the writer who inspired young William Faulkner and the model for his portrait of Colonel John Sartoris in *Flags in the Dust/Sartoris*—was, if not the owner of a plantation, a man who nevertheless "bought and sold slaves" (Williamson 1993, 33). Moreover, "The Falkner household in Ripley in the decade after 1851 was lightly unusual in that . . . in 1850 all of the slaves in the yard were black; in 1860 they were all mulatto" (23).

What that yard held in 1860, Williamson argues, was Colonel Falkner's own "shadow family"; that is, Faulkner's *own* ancestors practiced miscegenation. Colonel Falkner had at least one child, and probably more, by a black slave named Emeline, whom he had purchased, along with her family, for $900. Their daughter, Fannie Forrest Falkner, was named, Williamson speculates, for Frances, Falkner's favorite sister, and for Nathan Bedford Forrest, the Confederate leader who, at about the time of Fannie's birth, soundly defeated Union troops (in June 1864) in the Battle of Brice's Crossroads in central Mississippi. The evidence is circumstantial but telling. As Fannie came of age, Mrs. Falkner, giving no public reason other than her daughter's planning on college in Memphis, abruptly left her husband in Ripley and never returned.

In the fall of 1885 Fannie went off to the prestigious black Rust College in nearby Holly Springs, where Colonel Falkner had purchased property. Williamson writes, "Family tradition asserts that Colonel Falkner paid the bills. It also says that he frequently came to see his daughter in Holly Springs, and that when he did so he brought her flowers" (67). Furthermore, the 1880 census lists a single servant, Lena Falkner, living in the colonel's household on Ripley's Main Street. As Williamson notes, "She was thirteen years old and mulatto. It is possible that Lena was also Emeline's daughter, born about 1867, perhaps in Pontotoc, and that Colonel Falkner was her father" too (67). Faulkner's obsession with miscegenation in *Go Down, Moses*, then—his need, like Ike's, to understand it and, like Roth's, to respond to it—is urgently autobiographical. The urgency, in fact, may stem from a double cause. While it was not unusual to have a family record of miscegenation from the antebellum period, Faulkner also seems to have descended, on his mother's side, from a grandfather, Charlie Butler (his mother's father), the town tax collector of Oxford—who absconded with over $5,000 of the town's money and his mistress, the "beautiful octoroon" companion of Mrs. Jacob Thompson (Williamson 1993, 123). Thus, whereas the Falkner great-grandfather seems to have accepted responsibility for his black family, the Butler grandfather relinquished association with his white family.

Go Down, Moses is therefore a novel that is not so much an idyll about hunting experiences in the woods or a recollection of the past and present of other men's lives in Lafayette County as it is an investigation of William Faulkner's own inheritance. Like Ike McCaslin, Faulkner would bear no sons of his own; the white Faulkner line would be carried forward only through his brother John. Like Ike, Faulkner seems to have been deeply concerned, deeply anxious, about ancestors and descendants. Go Down, Moses is searingly powerful in large part because Faulkner is probing cultural questions that cut along his own bone and bloodline.

3

Further Grounds

The critical reception and history of Faulkner's *Go Down, Moses* is representative of critical response to his works generally—beginning with almost willful misunderstanding, and developing over time into a deeper understanding and clearer recognition of his accomplishment. Although George Marion O'Donnell, in the first significant work of criticism of Faulkner, had pointed out in 1939 that families and class were the dominant forces in his fiction,[22] and Conrad Aiken had praised Faulkner's pragmatic "method of *deliberately withheld meaning* (1939),[23] and Warren Beck had painstakingly pointed out Faulkner's techniques and their desirable effects (1941),[24] the first reviewers of *Go Down, Moses* nevertheless complained centrally about his style as unnecessarily difficult and obscurantist. Lionel Trilling's review of the novel for the *Nation* is representative: "Mr. Faulkner's literary mannerisms . . . are still dominant," he wrote, and continued, "the prose in which Mr. Faulkner renders . . . his stories is, to me, most irritating; it drones so lyrically on its way, so intentionally losing its syntax in its long sentences, so full of self-pity expressed through somniloquism or ventriloquism."[25] In London, a little more than four months later, an anonymous reviewer for the *Times Literary*

Supplement devoted much attention to what he considered Faulkner's "three characteristic failings," which he found to be "strongly in evidence" in *Go Down, Moses*: "his passion for bizarre or uncouth violences of situation. . . . his tortuous, tangential, elliptical style of narrative construction, . . . [a]nd . . . [his] prodigious, mountainous, dizzily soaring wordiness. This is his most intimidating vice."[26]

Even so, these reviewers found reason for praise. For Trilling, the episodes of *Go Down, Moses* "suggest more convincingly than anything I have read the complex tragedy of the South's racial dilemma" (Bassett, 297), and the London reviewer found chapter 3 of the novel, "Pantaloon in Black," to be "most impressive" (Bassett, 301). Both of them recognized what was new: Faulkner's insistently realistic depiction of plantation life and heritage. This is the point on which Malcolm Cowley began the first extended defense of Faulkner's work three years later, in 1945: "This legend of Faulkner's," he wrote, "is clearly not a scientific interpretation of Southern history (if such a thing exists); but neither is it the familiar plantation legend that has been embodied in hundreds of romantic novels. Faulkner presents the virtues of the old order as being moral rather than material. There is no baronial pomp in his novels; no profusion of silk and silver, mahogany and moonlight and champagne. The big house on Mr. Hubert Beauchamp's plantation . . . had a rotted floorboard in the back gallery that Mr. Hubert never got round to having fixed." Moreover, he continued, Faulkner's portrayal of race relations was just as realistic and revealing: "His attitude toward Negroes will seem surprising only to Northerners. It seems to have developed from the attitude of the slaveholders, which was often inhuman but never impersonal—that is, the slave might be treated as a domestic animal, but not as a machine or the servant of a machine. Apparently the slaveholding class had little or no feeling of racial animosity."[27]

Cowley's pioneering appreciation of the intent and thrust of Faulkner's fiction was praised by another Southern novelist, Robert Penn Warren, in 1946. In 1939 Warren had published his own historical fiction set in Kentucky, *Night Rider,* which concerns white vigilantes terrorizing blacks, and he confirmed the power of Faulkner's authenticity. "No land in all fiction," Warren wrote, "is more painstakingly analyzed from the sociological standpoint" than Faulkner's South. "The marks of class, occupation, and history are fully rendered and we know completely their speech, dress, food, houses, manners, and attitudes. Nature and sociology, geography and human geography, are scrupulously though effortlessly presented in Faulkner's work, and their significance for his work is very great."[28] As for race specifically, Warren noted,

> slavery, not the Negro, . . . is defined, quite flatly, as the curse, over and over again, and the Negro is the black cross in so far as he is the embodiment of the curse, the reminder of the guilt, the incarnation of the problem. That is the basic point. But now and then, as a kind of tangential irony, we have the notion, not of the burden of the white on the black, but of the burden of the black on the white, the weight of obligation, inefficiency, and so on, as well as the weight of guilt (the notion we find in the old story of the plantation mistress, who, after the Civil War, said: "Mr. Lincoln thought he was emancipating those slaves, but he was really emancipating me"). (324)

The black novelist and essayist Ralph Ellison published an essay in 1953 (but first written in 1946) that likewise cited the debate between Ike and Cass in the commissary in chapter 5 of *Go Down, Moses* as an exacting portrayal of the attitudes of the well-intentioned abolitionist in the South responding to the traditional Southern racist.[29]

NOVEL OR STORY COLLECTION?

None of the earliest responses took note of Faulkner's disapproval of his publisher's calling his 1942 novel *Go Down, Moses and Other Stories* or of the change in title. Initially, critics generally isolated "The Bear" for attention and analysis, ignoring its connections to the larger work about the McCaslins, Beauchamps, and Edmondses. In a major essay—cited as definitive from its publication in 1951 until the late 1970s—R. W. B. Lewis argued that "The Bear" could stand alone as a study of Isaac's rebirth in the woods. Herbert Perluck argued just as strongly that the scene of Ike in the commissary demonstrates that in the hunting episodes surrounding it in "The Bear," Ike has essentially failed, having learned nothing at all (see bibliography).[30]

Yet the necessary corrective readings, if unacknowledged at the time, began with Ursula Brumm, who wrote in 1955 that the novel was unified through the struggle of blacks and whites for ownership of the land,[31] and with Olga W. Vickery, who first noted in 1959 that the episodes were linked by the recurrent motif of the ritual hunt, by the concepts bondage and freedom, and by the notion of sacrifice.[32] For the most part, critics attempted to integrate episodes in the book by locating common themes, structural principles, or metaphors.

That all changed with the crucial essay of Stanley Tick in 1962. He argued more than unity in the novel; he argued that unless a reader saw *Go Down, Moses* as a single work where accumulative knowledge was vital and the recollection of all the episodes was necessary, the actual meaning would never be grasped at all:

> Let me give an instance of one of the relational ironies heretofore missed, as an indication of the extent of purposeful direction the full narrative possesses. The unnamed girl in "Delta Autumn" has borne a son to Carothers Edmonds; the time is 1940 (Ike, born in 1867, is here seventy-three). Edmonds repudiates both mother and child, though he leaves money to provide for them. Significantly, this fifth generation Edmonds is a "distaff" descendant of Lucius Quintus Carothers McCaslin, and the inheritor and possessor of the McCaslin land. Ironically, the girl reveals that she is a granddaughter of James Beauchamp (Tennie's Jim)—and thus even closer than Edmonds to the blood of old Lucius McCaslin, who is their common ancestor.
>
> At this point, information provided in three previous sections of *Go Down, Moses*—"Was," "The Fire and the Hearth," and "The Bear"—allows the reader of "Delta Autumn" to grasp the full extent of this irony, which is nothing less than a closing of the circle of racial evil. Like his ancient ancestor, Edmonds has committed miscegenation; like Lucius McCaslin, again, Edmonds refuses to acknowledge the child but instead offers a legacy anonymously.[33]

Tick finds another telling instance in the case of Butch Beauchamp:

> Directly relevant to "Delta Autumn" is the executed criminal in
> "Go Down, Moses"; his descent provides another relationship
> irony which must be comprehended. Samuel Worsham
> Beauchamp is a grandson of Lucas and Mollie, the child born to
> their eldest daughter, who, herself, did not survive the birth.
> Aware as the reader is now of the fate of the unnamed grand-
> daughter of James Beauchamp, we can appreciate the irony of
> making the executed criminal her second cousin. [Ike sends the
> granddaughter and baby back to Chicago, where Butch has just
> been executed.] The negro descendants of Eunice continue to be
> doomed. From the suicide of Eunice to the execution of Samuel
> and the rejection of the girl, none seems able to gain happiness.
> And the same is true for the white descendants that we know of.
> Only Lucas Beauchamp, in his isolating, Olympian pride, and
> Isaac in his Christ-like renunciation, are able to come to any sort
> of terms with their hostile environments. (331)

CRITICAL APPRAISAL

Other critics began following Faulkner's initial insistence (see chronology for 1949) and Tick's position. In 1963 Michael Millgate's long
exposition treated the novel as a singularly effective work.[34] In the same
year Cleanth Brooks's magisterial *William Faulkner* also addressed the
work by explicating each of the stories in the order of their presentation. In *The Tragic Mask* (also 1963), John L. Longley, Jr., stressed the
thematic interdependence between the wilderness and Ike's legacy, and
in the Summer 1967 issue of *Mississippi Quarterly* James M. Mellard
noted the unifying effect of a biblical rhythm in the work.

In many ways, the 1960s was an important decade for scholar-
ship on *Go Down, Moses*. Narrative perspective and its relationship to
the McCaslin chronology was examined by Thomas J. Wertenbaker,
Jr., in the December 1962 issue of *College English*, and in the Fall
1963 issue of *Studies in Short Fiction* Patrick G. Hogan, Jr., attempted

to draw out of the text the female McCaslin line. This period saw an increasing concern with the various textual versions of the novel in an attempt to understand the creation of the work and the progress of Faulkner's thought. Marvin Klotz's "Procrustean Revision in Faulkner's *Go Down, Moses*" in *American Literature* in March 1965 was followed by two book-length studies by Edward M. Holmes (1966) and Joanne V. Creighton (1977). This led, in turn, to a search for Faulkner's sources. Joseph Brogunier proposes one for the commissary entries in *Texas Studies in Literature and Language* (Summer 1972); Thomas L. McHaney locates a 1935 newspaper article on deer hunting in Mississippi in *Mississippi Quarterly* (Summer 1970); Calvin S. Brown recalls childhood experiences with Faulkner that are used in the novel in the *Georgia Review* (Winter 1966), and Elmo Howell in the January 1965 issue of *American Literature*, proposes an account of Indian funerals Faulkner may have seen. Some critics have compared Faulkner's novel to the work of other writers: William Pritchard to Joyce (1962), Donald G. Darnell to Cooper (1969), James Nagel to Twain (1969), Edwin M. Eigner to Melville (1969), Blanche Gelfant to Keats (1969), John M. Howell to Hemingway (1980), and John Colley to the more contemporary fiction of Vonnegut, Brautigan, and Coover (1981). Such analyses began to call Ike's heroism into question. In *English Studies* for February 1963 Richard E. Fisher noted "A sadly limited heroism"; John M. Muste detailed the failure of Ike's love in *Modern Fiction Studies* (Winter 1964–1965), and I began to question Ike's very possibilities for heroism in the *Southern Review* (Autumn 1970). In a pair of essays, Walter Taylor questioned Faulkner's understanding of the freedman generally and Rider particularly (*Ball State University Forum*, Winter 1967; *American Literature*, November 1972). Other critical judgments of Ike by Sanford Pinsker (1972) and J. Douglas Canfield (1980) were followed by Karl Zender's important essay on how to read "The Bear" in the first (and only) volume of *Faulkner Studies* (1980).

The detailed examinations of the novel in the 1980s began with my own work (1978), in which I described a phenomenological unity based on the various levels of narrative consciousness and perception, and by Susan Willis (1979), who, arguing from a Marxist viewpoint, saw the novel as an examination of hegemony and industrial capitalism (see bibliography). In 1983 Thadious Davis wrote from a black perspective that *Go Down, Moses* reveals Faulkner's recognition that history cannot be transcended (as Ike would wish) but instead must encompass the here and now; in the same year Walter Taylor wrote from a white perspective that the novel was part of Faulkner's lifelong struggle to understand the South.[35]

In many ways, John T. Matthews's 1982 reading, in which he sees the novel building with sophistication on the twin evils of possession—ownership of land and ownership of people—remains the most comprehensive treatment of the work and the most suggestive, and is worth quoting at some length.

> The complementary structure of *Go Down, Moses* . . . rests on a correspondence between the subjects of the first three stories and those of the wilderness trilogy.[36] Both "Was" and "The Old People" focus on a child's initiation into the fraternal brotherhood of hunters, and each contains the effort to enfranchise Ike with an account of his paternity and legacy. "The Bear" and "The Fire and the Hearth" share the chronicle of a hunt, the taking possession of one's patrimony, the sense of a better past drawing to its end, and the dilemma of choosing between the wilderness ethic and one's wife—a dilemma that demands some kind of renunciation. The pain of undeniable loss, the yearning for forgetfulness and release from consciousness, and the horror of endless grief draw "Pantaloon in Black" and "Delta Autumn" together; each imprisons its cot-bound mourner in a shower of tears, of grieving rain. . . . The first three stories involve black protagonists (Tomey's Turl, Lucas Beauchamp, and Rider), while the wilderness trilogy concentrates on Ike's career. Blackness (as "Pantaloon in Black" suggests) is not simply racial, of course; blackness represents social disenfranchisement, inarticulateness, and a tragic crisis that dissolves into comic treatment. . . . But *Go Down, Moses* also *disfigures* the lineal relations of its characters; Rider, for example, only rents land from a McCaslin, and the last story mentions Gavin Stevens' surprise at the discovery that Mollie Beauchamp and [Hamp] Worsham are sister and brother. It is as if the symmetry of the novel's biracial "family" is under the

> pressure of erasure or confusion, posing a deliberate indictment of
> old Carothers' untroubled, shortsighted segregation. The biologi-
> cal relationship of the novel's characters recedes before a centrifu-
> gal force. (219–20)

Later critical readings of the novel, including the best of them by
Michael Grimwood (1987) and Richard C. Moreland (1990), extend
these observations by Matthews (see bibliography). My recent collection of essays (1990) also builds on the premises underlying Matthews's
approach.

Still, this advanced criticism of the novel has not sufficiently
noticed what Lyall H. Powers in 1980 called the "special place" that
Go Down, Moses "occupies . . . among Faulkner's important works."
Powers refers to "The frame of specific temporary reference [that] is
further extended here than in all of his other major fiction." While
admitting that Faulkner follows "the familiar practice of the first dozen
years or so of the Yoknapatawpha Saga—that of doubling back over
ground already crossed in order to discover and examine the
antecedent cause of the growing evil already exposed," Powers claims
that *Go Down, Moses* "[goes] furthest into his characters' history, to
the virtual discovery of the New World; yet this novel bursts into our
own time, into the middle years (appropriately) of the Second World
War."[37] This singular comprehensiveness has been ignored, largely
because critics until now have followed Faulkner's presentation of
episodes, out of chronological order, and for all the ironies they have
discerned in those episodes, both independently and interrelated, they
have missed the chief ironies that become clear once we rearrange the
episodes and see what unfolds among them *simultaneously*—when we
note, for instance, that Ike's denial of his own grandfather's descendant occurs at the same time the town of Jefferson would deny any
relationship with Butch Beauchamp, or that Rider's death in Jefferson
is almost precisely contemporaneous with Butch's death in Chicago.

Yet these ironies—the deepest and darkest ironies of all in *Go
Down, Moses*—are just what the reader is expected, finally, to see.
These ironies are as striking and powerful as the insufficiency and the
communal fiction that ends *The Sound and the Fury*, in which tree and

signpost are unchanged, or the awareness that concludes *Absalom, Absalom!* when Shreve shows Quentin Compson that his love of the South must contain his hatred of parts of it. But the narratives of those two novels are chronological and explicit. In contrast, the narrative of *Go Down, Moses*—characterized by what might be called the miscegenation of time—is neither.

As the previous two chapters of this study indicate, the very centrality of events in *Go Down, Moses* to the life and belief of Faulkner and his ancestors seems to have kept Faulkner himself—like Quentin in the previous two novels—unable or unwilling to face the consequences of the South he was portraying. But Faulkner has provided us the material to understand that South in *Go Down, Moses*, and once we read the novel chronologically, some of those truths, at least, will be made much clearer. Attaining this sharpened focus through a fresh, chronological exploration of the book's events is what we now turn to in this reading.

A READING

4

Introduction

A great many readers are first introduced to Faulkner's work through the original four-part version of his story "The Bear," which he eventually expanded to five parts and incorporated into *Go Down, Moses*. A comparison of the two versions of "The Bear" reveals that in revising the story, Faulkner not only altered its length and structure; he also transformed its implications. In the same way, he continually altered *Go Down, Moses* throughout the book's construction. Indeed, the novel is unique in that it provides us insight, through Faulkner's changes of plan, into the development and evolution of his thoughts and attitudes; this in turn gives us clear directions on how we might most profitably read his work.

The shorter version of "The Bear" tells of young Isaac McCaslin's initiation into life through the boyhood ritual of the hunt. It shows that part of growing up is learning about death (in this case, the death of the bear Old Ben) and about the ending of important phases of life (symbolized by the invasion of industry and mercantilism through lumbering and the railway, which foretell the end of the Big Woods of Isaac's childhood). This shorter rendering of the story is at times idyllic. It very nearly takes the form of a parable; it is prevented from doing so only by the part-Indian character Boon Hogganbeck, whose madness is brought about by civilization's destroying the natural habitat where he found love, peace, and purpose. For the same reasons, civilization destroys Isaac's wise hunting tutor, Sam Fathers, the son of an Indian and a mulatto. Thus, in searching for the suitability of nostalgia, Faulkner flirts with sentimentality in this story. Only the irony of the last scene saves it. For this reason alone, Faulkner on occasion permitted the four-part version of "The Bear" to be reprinted or anthologized.

As for the chapter of *Go Down, Moses* called "The Bear," however, Faulkner never allowed separate publication.[38] That longer version of the story includes a special section in which Ike McCaslin traces his ancestry through commissary ledgers from the McCaslin plantation and through a discussion and debate with his cousin Cass. The entangling alliances that Ike discovers in his family's dark and previously hidden past show him that his own bloodline is characterized by the kind of miscegenation that produced Sam Fathers and severely limited Sam to a life of servitude. The ledger's records of the actions of earlier generations of McCaslins so taint the family name that Ike feels both the urgent responsibility to set things right and the urgent need to relinquish his past and his ancestors—to escape being a McCaslin as much as he can. Ike's very identity is ruptured by his confrontation with the family corruption—manifested first in acts of arrogant pride and full intention, then in the weak and cowardly dismissal of family legacy and responsibility. His immediate responses are narrated in this longer version of "The Bear," but the consequences stretch too far forward in time, just as the causes reach too far backward in time, for a short story to accommodate.

The fuller version of "The Bear"—more probing, more complex, more insecure—works on us (and is meant to work on us) very differently from the frequently anthologized shorter version. Readers who know only the original story will see, once they confront "The Bear" anew in *Go Down, Moses*, that even the happier moments of the shorter fiction are now deeply troubled and troubling. All the innocence is gone, even from the simplest childhood rite of initiation. Even the hunt itself has inescapably grim overtones. We need to ask, and we should ask, why this is so.

By tracing Faulkner's intense and obsessive need to shape *Go Down, Moses* as a novel of the McCaslin family that would illustrate the triumphs and tragic mistakes of plantation history in Mississippi, in many instances drawing on his own knowledge of what it means to inherit a family whose ancestors harbor the guilt of miscegenation, we can see how he deconstructed and rearranged the past in order to gain sufficient distance from it to write about it, yet remained close enough to his own regional and familial past to be absolutely true to the condition of the South in his own time. *Go Down, Moses* is Faulkner's fussiest novel. The decisions he made in choosing the book's characters and establishing their relationships to each other—something every novelist must do at the outset—show him struggling with more urgency and more anguish than he experienced at any other time in his career.

The genesis of *Go Down, Moses* is to be found in the story "Lion," published in 1935—Faulkner's first attempt to tell the hunting story encapsulated in "The Bear." He returned to "Lion" more than to any other work, changing it, revising it, and finally altogether transforming it. Using this same approach, he spent eight years shaping, reshaping, and reassembling the components of *Go Down, Moses*—more time than he spent on any other work except *A Fable* and *Snopes*, which are two and three times its length, respectively.

In conceiving and reconceiving "Lion," Faulkner caused Boon Hogganbeck to lose his grandmother, originally the niece of the Indian chief whose land he hunts. As Boon's ancestry was thus diminished, Sam Fathers's lineage was elevated: he became the chief's grandson. By the time Faulkner was writing "The Bear," which contains a reworking of "Lion," he changed his mind again, making Sam the son of the chief, now named Ikkemotubbe. The bloodline of Sam's mother was also raised: once a slave, she became a quadroon, which added white blood to her (and his) line. Sam's original name, Had-Two-Fathers (given to him in a short story called "A Justice"), had initially been derived from his mother's black husband and Indian lover. In "The Bear," in which Sam became the son of the chief and took on a chief's noble bearing, that name was inherited through the dim recesses of an Indian slaveowning past.

Already, Faulkner was developing some of the major representative characters of Yoknapatawpha County by deliberately complicating and obscuring their identities—partly by choice, partly through the accidental meetings and conditions of history, and always with the knowledge that racial identity can mark someone for life. Faulkner also began to transform his black characters by rereading the implications inherent in the story called "The Old People." There a minor figure, Jimbo, becomes the seed for James Beauchamp (Tennie's Jim), whose appearance is slight but whose impact is significant in the longer version of "The Bear."

The McCaslins developed over time, too, revealing how Faulkner used them to address and comprehend such representative settlers of Lafayette County as Washington Price in light of his own ancestry on both the Falkner and Butler sides. The first McCaslin to appear in Faulkner's fiction is Uncle Buck. In "Retreat" (first published in 1934; incorporated into *The Unvanquished* in 1938) Buck is the ultimate Confederate loyalist: he stops young Bayard in the square in Jefferson to shout his support of Bayard's father, Colonel John Sartoris. In a later appearance in *Absalom, Absalom!* (1936), he goes to Sutpen's Hundred for the burial of Charles Bon, claiming he would pray for any Confederate soldier, even a recruit from New Orleans whom he could not possibly have known. Then, in 1937, Faulkner gave Uncle Buck a twin brother, Uncle Buddy, who balances Buck's forthrightness with his shyness, and who serves as his brother's active counterpart by representing the McCaslin family in the war as a sergeant in Tennant's brigade in Virginia. Their joint defense of slavery—one by works, the other by deeds—meant that these characters had to own slaves. Faulkner confronted this in *The Unvanquished* through a sudden and remarkable digression: young Bayard Sartoris interrupts his own story to divulge that Uncle Buck and Uncle Buddy, having exchanged their plantation house for a slaves' cabin, lock the slaves into the plantation house by the front door at night, with the understanding that the slaves are to escape by the back door and be home by morning. The brothers remain deeply conflicted, then, about the practice of slavery, for they subscribe to the form of it, if not the spirit, well after the war. Faulkner made that observation, too, and he developed its implications in Buck and Buddy's conflicted reaction to slavery in "Was" at the opening of *Go Down, Moses*.

Colonel John Sartoris praises Uncle Buck and Uncle Buddy to young Bayard, noting that their bookkeeping system, by which the freed blacks nevertheless have to earn their freedom through labor, is an enlightened way to deal with emancipation. In *The Unvanquished* this is seen as positive and visionary; in the longer version of "The

Bear," which Faulkner wrote in 1941, the continuation of such a practice by Cass and Ike is seen as proof of the corrupting influence of slavery—of men "owning" and "freeing" other men. But that is not
Faulkner's first sense of Isaac McCaslin. Even before young Isaac took
the place of Quentin Compson in the reworking of "Lion" as part of
"The Bear," the older Ike was conceived for "Delta Autumn"—a man
still unable to face all the consequences of miscegenation and too
exhausted by his mistaken acts to exempt himself from its influence and
its taint.[39] The situation represented by Ike and Roth Edmonds in
"Delta Autumn" (1940), in which the family again commits acts of miscegenation, shows us that Faulkner's concern with race was growing
rapidly and had spread in time, through generations of the McCaslin
family, to encompass much of the history of Yoknapatawpha.

By 1941, then, Faulkner seems intractably haunted by the significance of racial history in the South and convinced that the McCaslin
family, through its various branches, would serve as a better fictional
vehicle for exploring the implications of race than had the Sartorises,
Compsons, or Sutpens—or even Joe Christmas in *Light in August*. That
this dominated his thinking is seen in the chart Faulkner drew when
transforming another short story, "Gold Is Not Always," into the second
episode of *Go Down, Moses*, "The Fire and the Hearth" (the original
drawing is now in the Alderman Library at the University of Virginia):

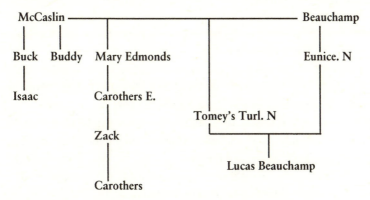

William Faulkner's genealogical chart of the McCaslin family.
*Courtesy William Faulkner Collections, Manuscripts Division, Special
Collections Department, University of Virginia Library.*

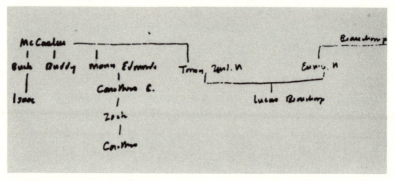

Faulkner's pencilled note showing the first stage of conceiving the McCaslins and Beauchamps.

Yet even this would change. Most important, Eunice Beauchamp, the legitimate full-blooded black mother of Lucas, was taken out of the Beauchamp family and made the mistress of Lucius Quintus Carothers McCaslin, who conceived by her a daughter, Tomasina (called Tomey), and then by that daughter a son, Terrel (Tomey's Turl). In time—in the novel, in the gap of undescribed time just after "Was"— Tomey's Turl marries Tennie Beauchamp, a black slave who, according to custom, has taken as her last name that of her white owner, Hubert Beauchamp; it is through Tennie that the name of Faulkner's Beauchamp line finally begins. In the novel, Lucas is the youngest surviving child of Tomey's Turl and Tennie; he is preceded by three children who die young and then by a brother, James, and a sister, Sophonsiba (later Fonsiba).

The Beauchamp family had been the Prim family in an earlier draft, and their plantation, Warwick, had been called Primrose. By replacing the plantation's quaint Southern name with that of a well-known castle and family in England, Faulkner established a way to measure, through the Beauchamps' borrowing a name they could not sustain, the deterioration of the Beauchamp line. The sharp decline in the fortunes of the Beauchamps is later verified and furthered in "The Bear," when Sophonsiba returns to Warwick to find that Hubert has taken a black mistress from the plantation—thus, in his hapless way, imitating old L. Q. C. McCaslin.

46

Introduction

It is important to note that Faulkner did not change every family line in reaction to his growing recognition of the effects of race. For instance, he made no adjustments to the McCaslin bloodline or to the Edmonds line, derived from the marriage of L. Q. C. McCaslin's daughter. But he changed the black line considerably, and that is important too. Descending from McCaslin's daughter Tomey, all the Beauchamps had mixed blood. The pure black line, that is, became mulatto: at some point, even Sam Fathers, hovering like a spirit at the side of the young Isaac McCaslin, was changed from an Indian to a mixed son of an Indian and a mulatto. The point is stark and, for Faulkner, clearly unavoidable: miscegenation is the very heart of the McCaslin story and the central theme of *Go Down, Moses*; like the leitmotiv of a symphony, it holds all the movements, or episodes, together.

Analysis of the tangled history of Faulkner's conceptualization of his novel is a fundamental key to reading and understanding it, for it shows Faulkner doing exactly what his characters are made to do: to confront the inescapable and irrevocable realities of race and miscegenation by conflictual acceptance and avoidance. Faulkner himself was undergoing the unsettled responses to race that mark the psychological development of his characters and their interactions in the novel. Understanding that the basic movement of *Go Down, Moses* is a continual wavering between acceptance and avoidance aids the reader immeasurably.

Of the numerous key changes Faulkner made during the long and torturous gestation of *Go Down, Moses*, there is one that Eric J. Sundquist finds "nothing short of madness" (131). Faulkner transformed a character originally named Henry Coldfield Sutpen (born of the interbreeding of Thomas Sutpen and his black slave Rosa) into Lucas's mulatto grandson Butch Beauchamp, the central subject of "Go Down, Moses." Thus, even as he was composing *Absalom, Absalom!* between 1934 and 1936, Faulkner was focused on miscegenation. In that novel, various characters find narrative strategies to avoid confronting cruel acts of racial dominance and submission. The characters in *Go Down, Moses*, however, are not given that luxury. For them, miscegenation is linked, through bloodlines, to ancestry and inheritance—as it might have been for Faulkner if he had just then learned of his own ancestral history of miscegenation. This makes *Go Down, Moses* a novel that is more intense, more singular, and more personal.

Miscegenation is thematic in *Go Down, Moses*; it is a chief means of character delineation. It is also a chief means of structuring the novel, and frequently metaphoric. According to Sidney Kaplan, who conducted pioneering historical research on miscegenation,[40] the word was first coined by the anonymous authors of a 72-page racist pamphlet—which pretends to be abolitionist while actually supporting racism—traces the formative roots of two neologisms for racial mixing between blacks and whites: "The first [is] *miscegenation* (from the Latin *miscere*, to mix, and *genus*, race) with its derivatives, *miscegen, miscegenate* and *miscegenetic*; the second—a more precise neologism—is *melaleukation* (from the Greek *melas*, black, and *leukos*, white) with its derivatives, *melaleukon* and *melaleuketic*" (Kaplan: 277–78).

Applied to bloodlines, the term denoted blending or mixing—and, in due course, carried connotations of diluting, obscuring, mixing up. Faulkner used this idea on a structural level in *Go Down, Moses* by blending or mixing up the families and their stories, as well as his presentation of them. By 1940 he had already had success at building novels by combining shorter works of fiction (often previously published short stories). This approach had worked especially well for him in *The Unvanquished* (1938) and helped him to put together—to compose—*The Hamlet* (1940). In 1940 he told Random House of his plan to use this technique in *Go Down, Moses*. In constructing that novel, however, Faulkner departed from his previous pattern of chronology and sequence.

The Unvanquished, while a novel of recollection, nevertheless depends on Bayard's remembering his growing up in the historical order of events. Even in earlier and more experimental works, such as *The Sound and the Fury* (with its single, designated flashback in part 2), *As I Lay Dying* (with its multiple narrators and narrative perspectives), and *Sanctuary* (with its multiple settings and family lines—Drakes, Benbows, Goodwins), Faulkner kept to a fundamental chronology. In *Absalom, Absalom!*—perhaps his most experimental novel—he made a point of chronology, of the vital role of sequence as a means of explanation and understanding. Yet in *Go Down, Moses*, even though explanation and understanding were presumably what he was after, Faulkner scrambled chronology and sequence.

Nearly all published studies of *Go Down, Moses* examine the novel according to the order of its episodes, implying, if not actually arguing, the value and significance of their sequence—for instance, the presentation of "Pantaloon in Black" (a story of the present time) before "The Old People" (one of the stories set in the previous century). Yet an unquestioning acceptance of the novel's structure obscures the actual causes and consequences of events. Such a reading does not deny or eliminate events, but it fails to uncover relationships among them that are revealed when those events are temporally unscrambled. For example, one significant matter about "Pantaloon in Black," the story of Rider's lynching, is that it is almost precisely contemporary not with the deer hunt that follows it in the book but with the execution of Butch Beauchamp, which comes at the very end of the novel. Both episodes are contemporary with the novel's publication and with each other: the execution up North, the lynching down South.

Unscrambling the peculiar mixture or blending of presentation, the miscegenation of time and episode in *Go Down, Moses*, allows a recharting of events in the chronological order of their occurrence (see Appendix I). We see that three generations of McCaslins play off four generations of Edmonds (so that Ike lives through the management of the McCaslin plantation by Cass, Zack, and Roth) and six generations of Beauchamps (so that Ike arrives in the generation following the one instructed by old McCaslin's legacy and lives to see its effects on three more generations of descendants, including the grandchild of Tennie's Jim). Thus it becomes clear that the ritual hunts of the Beauchamps and of Sam and Ike are temporally distant from the scenes that take place in 1940.

Faulkner's use of deconstruction, which leads the reader to events along chronological lines, has long been recognized as one of his basic narrative strategies (Aiken; Kinney, 1978; Matthews; Snead; Sundquist). Unscrambling his deliberately obscuring presentation not only points to the force of juxtapositions that Faulkner meant his readers to sense, if not see; it also gives a particular premium to certain events and a privileging to certain characters.

49

Ritual hunts, the McCaslin ledgers, and a crime-ridden present emerge as the three central emphases in the three time periods addressed in this study: the period before the Civil War (covered in chapter 5, "Was"); the period following the Civil War (chapter 6, "Then"); and the period around World War II, which is the present time of the novel and the time of its publication (chapter 7, "Now"). It becomes apparent that the perspectives that best inform us of those times are not those of the white characters, who often fail to recognize events for what they are or what they might become, but those of the blacks: Tomey's Turl and Sam Fathers in the antebellum period; Lucas and his siblings in the post–Civil War period known as Reconstruction; and Rider, Butch Beauchamp, and the granddaughter of Tennie's Jim in 1940, the novel's present. The black characters most help the reader to measure the price of past deeds in Yoknapatawpha and their cost to those yet living there; they suggest the whites' need for rationalization and obscurity; and they justify Molly's final gospel call in chapter 7.

Reestablishing the chronological sequence of the events in *Go Down, Moses* not only discloses their meaning, which Faulkner simply implies; it also demands the reader's active involvement in arranging and rearranging those events thus releasing the power of one of the most forceful novels of twentieth-century America.

5

Was
(1859–1883)

Best go back to the beginning. At least as far back as history will take me. Back to the land of the Choctaws, the land of my own birth. I remembered a historical marker on the edge of my father's farm in Amite County, Mississippi. It is on Highway 24, between McComb and Liberty, six counties south of Holmes. I had paid it no mind; just another marker for geriatric tourists from up North to stop and read. I knew it had something to do with the Choctaw Nation.

My father was beyond ninety and in rapidly declining health. I would begin there. Perhaps he knew stories. His mind was still clear. At least I could read the sign.

It would be the first of many trips I would make, by car, bus, and airplane, in search of the original owners of Section Thirteen, people I should have known but didn't.

I found my father sitting on the front porch of his farmhouse, the same house I was born in sixty-five years earlier. A few hundred yards from where he had been born and raised.

After a brief visit, we fell to talking about the old days. I recalled that the county I intended to write about, Holmes, had been named for David Holmes, governor of the Mississippi territory when my father's people arrived from Georgia and later first governor of the state of Mississippi. He was not a peaceful man. Our county, Amite, had been named by the French because of the cordial reception the

Choctaw Indians had given them. *Amite.* While the word was in my mind, I went inside and checked the ragged old dictionary our father had bought when his children were young.

Amity n., pl. -ties. Peaceful relations, as between nations; friendship. (Middle English *amite*, from Old French *amitie*, from Medieval Latin *amīcitās* from Latin *amīcus*, friend.)

Reading the definition gave me a soothing, warm feeling. Yes, yes. That is what the old man sitting on the front porch is like. Yes, yes. We of Amite County have always been a people of amity. Quickly the thought of ghastly violence during the sixties against black people in our county who wanted to register to vote flushed the notion from my head. Back outside I asked my father if there had been any Indians in this neighborhood when he was a boy. He said he didn't remember any. He did, however, recollect his mother and grandfather talking about the Indians. They had encountered many along the way from Georgia. And here as well.

"Were they friendly?"

"Oh yes. They said they were as nice as they could be. Never gave them any trouble. Said they helped them get settled when they got here." The feeling of *amīcitās* came back for a moment.

I asked him if he would like to ride up the road with me, that I wanted to read what was on the historical marker. He went inside, got his hat, and we got in the car. As I started the engine he said, "Of course, you know I'm like Grandpa Bunt, always ready to burn the other fellow's gasoline. But far as that's concerned, I can tell you what's on the marker if that's all you want to know."

I turned the motor off and got my pen as he recited the exact wording:

CEDED BY CHOCTAWS AND CHICKASAWS
IN FORT ADAMS TREATY, 1801,
CONFIRMING EARLIER BRITISH
TREATY. CONTAINED MOST OF
PRESENT WARREN, JEFFERSON,
CLAIBORNE, ADAMS, FRANKLIN,
WILKINSON, AND AMITE COUNTIES.

"Is that it?" I asked.

"Well, up at the top it says, 'Old Natchez District.' And an outline map of Mississippi. Down at the bottom it says, 'Mississippi Historical Commission. Nineteen fifty-two.'"

—Campbell, 25–27

Go *Down, Moses* begins chronologically with events "out of the old time, the old days" (4) between 1859 and 1883. In each episode of this period—in "Was," "The Old People," and sections 1, 2, and 3 of "The Bear"—ritual hunting is seen both as a game and as a process of maturation by which McCaslin Edmonds (Cass) and Ike McCaslin come to understand human nature and, more important, the burden of history in sharply discrepant ways. Yet for both, the joys of childhood—rendered by Faulkner in both happy and somber spirit—are based on an innocence that knowledge will betray: an innocence explicitly about race and freedom. The lessons the two cousins learn, in the crowded events of hunting as a game or race, reflect the larger lessons about race and freedom that the South learned in the course of the War Between the States. The contest between man and beast is meant to displace—but never with complete success—the larger deadly contest of man against man, of brother against brother. W. J. Cash has argued that such contests were bred on the plantations because the planters themselves came from the heritage of crude frontier life:

> [T]he planters [had] virtually unlimited sway over their bondsmen, and the natural effect on the common whites of the example of these planters . . . eventuated in this: that the individualism of the plantation world would be one which, like that of the backcountry before it, would be far too much concerned with bald, immediate, unsupported assertion of the ego, which placed too great stress on the inviolability of personal whim, and which was full of the chip-on-the-shoulder swagger and brag of a boy—one, in brief, of which the essence was the boast, voiced or not, on the part of every Southerner, that he would knock hell out of whoever dared to cross him. This character is of the utmost significance. For its corollary was the perpetuation and acceleration of the tendency to violence which had grown up in the Southern back-

woods as it naturally grows up on all frontiers. (*The Mind of the South*, 42–43)

All of these observations are central to the early period of *Go Down, Moses*; there are ways in which violence underscores the bragging of Uncle Buck or Hubert Beauchamp in "Was," just as there is bragging in the hunts of the later episodes, all of which grow out of egos surging toward dominance through violence at the expense of both animals and men.

The earliest story of the novel is "Was," the story of a runaway slave and the attempt to recapture him. In its larger outlines, the narrative traces a very real problem in the Old South between 1851 and the outbreak of the Civil War: the problem of runaway slaves. Drew Gilpin Faust, who has studied how the problem affected James Henry Hammond's plantation in South Carolina, Silver Bluff, between 1831 and 1855, learned that no single escape from that plantation was ever successful. Of the 37 slaves involved—most of them newly purchased—roughly two-thirds were captured, and one-third returned voluntarily, often because of bad weather or lack of provisions.[41] Next to such stark realities—the urgency for freedom, the need to keep control; fear, anguish, near-starvation—"Was" seems high-spirited and comic. Drawing on the tall tale of the frontier rather than on its hardships, delighting in the humor of hyperbole and the plot devices of shrewdness and ingenuity, it seems more related to such folk tales as "The Big Bear of Arkansas" by Thomas Bangs Thorpe (a tale that does hold similarities to parts of "The Bear").[42] But the hunt in "Was," like the hunts in all the early episodes of *Go Down, Moses*, is sharply controlled by implicit and explicit irony and by an accumulation and juxtaposition of suggestive details that constantly counter or even undermine the surface narration.

"Was" begins with an indoor chase involving a loose fox and some noisy dogs. As Cass recalls years later for his cousin Ike (who was not yet born at the time of the incident, when Cass was nine years old), Uncle Buck—having just discovered the black slave Tomey's Turl has run away from the plantation again—learns that at the same time, the caged fox in his kitchen has escaped. Buck's brother, Uncle Buddy, begins his own room-to-room race to recapture the fox—which is already being pursued by a bunch of barking dogs—with the aid of some lumber from a stack of firewood. The comedy of the scene derives in part from its sheer chaos and in part from the fact that Uncle Buddy, who is always a good poker player but never a good hunter, is unable to stop any of the animals from disrupting the cabin he keeps so fastidiously clean.

In two ways, Faulkner's guarded presentation of this opening slapstick performance raises questions about its real significance. First, the story is told by the elderly bachelor Cass many years after the event (nearly a half-century later) to his cousin, now known as Uncle Ike— an old widower who is "uncle to half a county and father to no one" (3). That is, the story is given importance, but it is told to a strange audience—a man who has no family and no slaves and who is subjected to a partial account based on Cass's distant childhood memory. Second, Cass apparently has never perceived the analogy between Tomey's Turl and the fox. Yet Cass's tale, as it unfolds, continues to underscore the analogy between animals and people—illustrated, for example, by the wiliness, or "foxiness," of Uncle Buck in his hunt for Tomey's Turl, as well as that of Sophonsiba Beauchamp in her parallel hunt for Uncle Buck.

Much of the comedy in "Was" stems not from young Cass's innocence but from Uncle Buck's: he is as naive before Sophonsiba later in the story as he is before Uncle Buddy as he prepares to set out with Cass to hunt for Tomey's Turl. In each case, Uncle Buck's attention is focused only on the chase itself and on the ritual that makes it not only a "proper" chase but a game. Thus, nearly unconsciously, he puts on a tie for the event, because he will meet a lady in the course of it, and he means to be both a hunter and a gentleman—a combination he will not be able to manage very well. Then, rather than beginning the hunt without delay, he sits down to breakfast with his brother in order to give Tomey's Turl a better head start: he wants a sporting match.

Years later, Uncle Buck's innocence is matched by that of Cass, who fails to see that in giving the story to Ike as he does, he is only underscoring Uncle Buck's and Uncle Buddy's position on *race* (as well as Hubert Beauchamp's). The hunt makes the word a homonym: the chase becomes inseparable from skin color, which distinguishes the hunter from the hunted, and by which slaves are made possessions, like the fox, and so more animal than human. Cass's shortsightedness, both as a boy observing the action and as an adult telling the story of it, makes "Was" openly ironic from the start. Throughout, Cass says things he does not know he is saying. Our job as readers is to determine whether he senses more than he is telling—and to discern what Ike is actually hearing.

Cass explains that Tomey's Turl's escape happens each spring, when he feels the urge to see Tennie, a female slave on the neighboring plantation. Uncle Buck could resolve this problem by purchasing Tennie for Tomey's Turl, but he complains that he has too many blacks on his land already (and, we know, he really wants to make the annual hunt). Tennie's owner, Hubert Beauchamp, head of the neighboring plantation, refuses to buy Tomey's Turl; moreover, he says he would not want "that damn white half-McCaslin" (6) even if he cost him nothing. The remark is matter-of-fact to Cass, but it stands out as the only remark in the entire account that makes it clear that Uncle Buck is about to chase down his own half-brother, not as family but as property, and he has insisted that he will do so each year. It soon becomes clear that he cannot afford to have Hubert Beauchamp catch Tomey's Turl and return him, because if he did so he would bring along his unmarried sister, Sophonsiba—and Uncle Buck himself would become the quarry, the object of the game. Tomey's Turl's escape means that both he and Uncle Buck, both the black and white half-brothers, are at risk. What they stand to gain or lose is also the same: their freedom.

Uncle Buddy's dismay over the loose fox is indicative of his larger distrust of his brother. As Cass leaves to accompany Uncle Buck on the hunt for Tomey's Turl, Uncle Buddy warns him to watch Uncle Buck. The warning is a wise one. What follows is Uncle Buck's hapless attempt to flush Tomey's Turl by entering woods that apparently run alongside the open ground over which the runaway slave has ridden. When Uncle Buck exits the woods whooping, giving away his own position, he makes the chase a traditional sporting match—but also a futile one (8). This is his first major mistake, because it allows Tomey's Turl time to reach Tennie and thus forces Uncle Buck to go onto Beauchamp land.

Cass's description of the Beauchamp plantation is similar to his description of the McCaslin place: both are run-down and seedy. The Beauchamp home, however, has greater pretensions. Someone—probably Miss Sophonsiba—has named it Warwick, after an English manor house, and Sophonsiba works mightily to realize that status for the plantation. Her positioning a boy at the gatepost to announce Uncle Buck's arrival by blowing a fox-horn (clearly, she has been expecting him) seems out of place in light of our first view of Mr. Hubert, who is found sitting in the springhouse, soaking his feet and drinking a toddy (9), yet Cass fails to see any discrepancy. Nor does Cass realize, until much later, that Miss Sophonsiba did not welcome them immediately upon their arrival because she was upstairs preparing herself for Uncle Buck's visit by putting on her fine dress, her jewelry, and perfume.

Warwick is thus a divided household, as the McCaslins' is: Miss Sophonsiba struggles to bring form and manners to the Old South, while her brother is content to sit and drink; Uncle Buddy attempts to maintain traditional order, while Uncle Buck seems only to disrupt it. In "Was" Faulkner shows two early ways of life clashing through the "agrarian" Miss Sophonisba's attempts to tame and conquer the frontier hunting life of her brother, which has come to dominate the McCaslins as well. The McCaslins, like her brother, need her. (In time, we will learn, she marries Uncle Buck, restructures the McCaslin plantation during a foreshortened life, and gives birth to Ike; Cass, again innocently, is telling part of the story of the courtship of Ike's parents.) Cass does not seem to recognize the implications of his story for Ike, who has doubtless heard it before, as Cass was only nine years old when the events took place. But later, by the time of part 4 of "The Bear," Ike will have taken Sophonsiba's attitude as his own. His life will have become economic responsibility and plantation management, keeping order through good supervision and good ledgers—not the life of the frontier hunter. Thus, Ike will have become a former hunter, mourning Sam Fathers.

Nor does Cass sense the conspiracies afoot, as we are meant to see. Mr. Hubert offers Uncle Buck help in hunting Tomey's Turl, but offers him a drink first—and Uncle Buck, attuned to Hubert's style of life, agrees. That Miss Sophonsiba makes the drink for Uncle Buck with considerable social ritual (12) and then offers him another one after his nap (13)—both in clear sight of Hubert, who seems not to take a drink himself—not only suggests that Uncle Buck becomes sufficiently inebriated to have additional difficulty in capturing Tomey's Turl (eventuating in his having to spend the night at Warwick) but also suggests collusion between brother and sister. Hubert's willingness to wager Uncle Buck that he will need to spend the night (16) points both to his deceitful intention and to Uncle Buck's muddled mind.

But Hubert and Sophonsiba's scheme is not the only conspiracy in play. Cass (unlike Uncle Buck) has no difficulty at all finding Tomey's Turl while Hubert and Uncle Buck nap after dinner, and Tomey's Turl reveals that he, too, has a secret plan (12–13). He has made an analogy himself: he knows he wants Tennie, and he senses that Sophonsiba wants Uncle Buck. His coded comment to Cass—"'anytime you wants to git something done . . . just get the women-folks to working at it'" (13)—means that Miss Sophonsiba (and perhaps Tennie) is in partnership with Tomey's Turl. And why not? For if Sophonsiba conquers Uncle Buck, Tomey's Turl can settle down with Tennie. The springtime hunts are not a game for Tomey's Turl, as they are for Uncle Buck.

The comedy of "Was," then, springs from the ways in which the multiple plots coordinate and conflict with one another as they simultaneously unfold. Our early awareness of plot and counterplot, in fact, allows us to see parallels that pass by Uncle Buck and Cass. For example, Uncle Buck's failure to flush his half-brother from one of the cabins at Warwick precedes Sophonsiba's far more successful plan to trap Uncle Buck. If Uncle Buck inadvertently lets Tomey's Turl escape because he forgets what every good hunter knows—that when flushing a black, one should stand to the side of the door and not in front of it (18)—he forgets too that the hunter often snares the quarry where the hunted least expects it. Clearly, what Sophonsiba does on the second floor of her plantation home is to move from the front room, where the family normally sleeps, to one of the back rooms usually reserved for guests. She temporarily suspends her sense of aristocratic propriety to use the principle of entrapment associated with the frontiersman and the hunter. She thus makes the hunter and the hunted one, and so beats Uncle Buck at his own game. As Hubert himself notes, good hunters in animal country do not lie down in the dens of animals they know to be nearby (21). That Faulkner means Sophonsiba's hunt to be equated with Uncle Buck's—making the two McCaslins, one white, the other black, quarries—is underlined by Hubert's comment that Uncle Buck has run a good, hard race but has lost (22).

Some tall tales would end at this point, with the smart player outsmarted at his own game. But the principle of the tall tale, hyperbolic ingenuity, can be extended, making the tall tale even taller, longer, and more successful. Hubert, we learn, is as discontented with success as Uncle Buck is with defeat. He would like to rid himself of Tennie as well as Sophonsiba and so be rid of McCaslins forever. Hubert reminds Uncle Buck of the $500 bet he has won because Uncle Buck and Tomey's Turl did not return to their home by midnight (16, 22). He offers Uncle Buck a new sporting chance: to transfer the verbal bet to a poker game, for which he will renegotiate the terms. Once more, the equations in the story change. Hubert says he will bet his newly won $500 against his sister. The holder of the lowest hand in a five-card draw will "win" Sophonsiba and will purchase the black he does not already own for $300. For Uncle Buck, losing the poker game—and thus taking Sophonsiba as his wife and buying Tennie—is the only way to hold on to some of his money. For Hubert, winning the game is a way to rid himself of both sister and slave; should he lose, he will still be ahead $200. Neither of them is concerned that they are turning two courtships into a gamble based on economic greed; neither is concerned that they are dehumanizing both Sophonsiba and the mulatto—Beauchamp sister and McCaslin half-brother—by making them the stakes in the game.

While the presentation of the game is elliptical—although young Cass deals, he clearly does not comprehend the hands dealt and played—it seems clear that in the first deal, Hubert receives two pairs, fives and kings, and discards one card, hoping to get three of a kind. He does; he is jubilant; he calls and wins. That we can determine what is happening while the boy Cass cannot shows us that we must probe and perhaps reinterpret everything the elderly Cass says in recounting the story for Ike (and us).

In desperation after losing the game, Uncle Buck slips Cass out of a window early the next morning to race home and fetch Uncle Buddy. Uncle Buck's own canniness is openly crude next to the actions of Hubert, Tomey's Turl, and Sophonsiba—an indication that all of his decisions in this story may have been wrong ones.

Uncle Buddy, on the other hand, is not as easily fooled as Uncle Buck. When he arrives at Warwick, he will not drink. He too plays a game of poker with Hubert, but finds a way to renegotiate the terms in his own favor. If Hubert wins, he will be exempted from his earlier promise to give Uncle Buck land and slaves as Sophonsiba's dowry (25), and he will still retain the $300 for Tennie while ridding himself of her and Tomey's Turl. Again, though, Hubert stands to win something even if he loses. For Uncle Buddy, winning the game is the only way to rescue his brother from marriage, so the generosity of his offer is unavoidable. What Uncle Buddy gambles on initially, then, is his seductive choice of stakes and his superiority at playing poker.

Once the game is under way, Uncle Buddy interrupts it to propose new stakes (26–27) that end the risk of any payment by Hubert for Tomey's Turl. Much of Uncle Buddy's gamesmanship is not in the cards (just as much of Uncle Buck's was not in actually chasing down and capturing Tomey's Turl) but in outmaneuvering the opponent. Hubert senses that he is being outflanked and stops the game momentarily to review the stakes with Uncle Buddy before they proceed any further (27). Hubert's hesitation shows us that Uncle Buck is as enslaved as Tomey's Turl. And such a complicated wager—despite the false freedom it seems to award Hubert, who chooses to call off the game before the hands are fully played out—puts risk on both sides.

No longer at risk, though, is Tomey's Turl; while remaining a slave, he will be free to join Tennie, no matter who wins. Throughout the story, the actions of Tomey's Turl have bespoken a superb "double consciousness"; his white blood, perhaps, has helped him to sense the white man's interests and predispositions. He sensed them when Uncle Buck was standing in front of the doorways of Tennie's cabin and thus was able to knock him down and escape; now he stands at the doorway to Mr. Hubert's house, and thus he is on hand to deal the cards. Having won Tennie, his choice now is where they will both live. Again, hunter and hunted are one, but this time it is Tomey's Turl, not Uncle Buck—and Tomey's Turl wins.

The superior if necessary shrewdness of those who are caged is given a minor reprise to make the point clear (28–29), but the black's superiority to the whites is not the primary value advocated in "Was." Humanity is. What remains unspoken is the real motivation of Uncle Buck and Uncle Buddy. Their desperate chase for their half-brother and the subsequent poker game arise not merely from a desire to hold on to their property; they arise from their fear that Tomey's Turl's freedom will result in a fruitful marriage with Tennie that will continue the black McCaslin line. In harboring Tomey's Turl, they also harbor the guilt and shame they have inherited through their father's miscegenation, while allowing his freedom will only result in compounding that act of miscegenation. Buck and Buddy clearly plan to expiate their blood guilt by remaining celibate and by forcing Tomey's Turl to remain celibate too. Sophonsiba's need is likewise partly unspoken; she wants not simply to get married but to make a good match. In a strange and telling way, her own concern about the economics (as well as the customs) of marriage is represented by her taking on monetary value herself as part of a wager in a series of poker games.

Buck and Buddy and Sophonsiba all thus portray in "Was" those values assigned to genealogy and inculcated in an antebellum South that was still just at the edges of a newly settled frontier—and such values severely proscribe any easy way to make "the old time, the old days" nostalgic. Tomey's Turl is wiser than any of them, despite his restricted role in the culture. What he yearns for, bargains for, and gambles for is Tennie. His interest, unlike the interests of all the adult white characters, is simply unfettered love that humanizes the object, rather than manipulation that objectifies humanity. Tomey's Turl's maneuvers are all motivated by human passion and by love for someone else, not by the ego that Cass sees as characterizing the white frontiersman and plantation owner. This lesson is one that none of the adult McCaslins and Beauchamps seems to understand.

We should remember, however, that "Was" is not a story told in the present but a story of past events deliberately framed by Cass and told to his cousin Ike years later. By then, we are reminded, Cass, who is 16 years older than Ike, has been more like a brother than a cousin to Ike—indeed, more like a surrogate father to him (4). Cass is a member of the distaff side of the family (3), and so is freed from the taint of miscegenation. He tells the story to Ike not out of pride but out of a desire to instruct. In choosing celibacy for himself and in repudiating his own inheritance of miscegenation at this later time, Ike is unintentionally imitating the Uncle Buck and Uncle Buddy of this story. This is a situation he should wish to escape, not foster. But Cass's lesson fails.

Much later, in chapter 6 of *Go Down, Moses*, "Delta Autumn," we will see how deeply Ike fails to understand. His reaction to Roth's mistress counters the humanity represented by Tomey's Turl (and, by implication, Tennie) in "Was," a story that took place before Ike was born—a story involving a visit by Uncle Buck (who would later become Ike's father) to Warwick, which would lead to his marriage to Sophonsiba and then to Ike's own birth.

After "Was," *Go Down, Moses* continues to provide Cass with opportunities to teach Ike. One important thread that connects the hunting stories in the first time period of the narrative is Cass's repeated attempts to play father to Ike: to teach him about the visionary deer at the close of "The Old People" and to teach him once more when Old Ben dies in "The Bear." In "Was," Tomey's Turl is the one with vision, but only Cass will finally come to recognize it.

Faulkner deliberately begins "The Old People" in imitation of the Book of Genesis: darkness turns slowly to light; voices are heard. Sam Fathers is standing behind Isaac (now 10 years old); then a buck appears (157). This is a visionary, incandescent moment in 1877—17 years after Tomey's Turl managed to secure Tennie through a white man's poker game. He has long been married to Tennie, and they have six children, three of them still living. Uncle Buck and Uncle Buddy have both died, and with the death of his mother earlier that year, Isaac had witnessed Cass taking over the family plantation. Isaac is in need of a parent, and he has found one in Sam Fathers, whom he deeply loves—a former slave of the McCaslins who is part white, part black, part Indian. Isaac and Sam are united through Sam's love of the woods and of freedom (at the cost of responsibility). Like the later Ike, Sam cares little for property and is childless. More important, they are both childlike, their contentment actually stemming from the kind of self-satisfaction that Cass saw at the start of Southern white settlement.

In their shared childlike innocence, Sam and Isaac share the vision of the deer. Sam is in the process of teaching Isaac how to hunt, as his father had taught him, as Isaac manages to shoot the deer without even realizing it. He continues to follow Sam's instructions, hooking his fingers in the deer's nostrils, pulling his head back, and slitting his throat with a knife Sam hands to him. Sam completes what is clearly an initiation rite for the hunter by wiping the buck's blood on the boy's face. Without the benefit of any narrative frame, it is hard at first to say whether this bloody death following a splendid vision is a mystical rite of initiation that we should appreciate or a brutal killing that is not necessary to preserve any life. Coming to this episode directly after "Was," we may wish to be cautious about judging its significance too quickly. Ike himself is not troubled; for him, killing the buck is an accomplishment that makes him feel both joy and humility (159). At one with the buck, Isaac is also at one with Sam Fathers. Later, we are told, still under Sam's tutelage, Isaac learns to love the woods: although they are awesome to him—alive, huge (169)—they are not fearsome; they are transcendent. Thus, attuning himself to Sam and to the woods, even at the expense of his home and family on the plantation, Isaac feels himself maturing and his values deepening.

"The Old People"—a story that begins with a vision of a buck during the apparent beginning of time, if not of the world—ends with a similar vision of a buck, but one that is special, moving effortlessly past and beyond Isaac and Sam, pausing only briefly before disappearing, as Sam—meaning not to kill him but to preserve him—remarks, almost worshipfully, "'Oleh, Chief . . . Grandfather'" (177). These mysterious, even mystical words from another language and attitude render the final passage of "The Old People" less ambivalent than its beginning. Sam and Isaac respect this buck and appreciate its beauty; they do not interrupt it, kill it, or exploit it, as they had arguably done earlier to the other buck as the price of initiating Isaac into the life of the Big Woods.

Even so, there are other, disturbing elements in the story. Just after Ike's initiation and his identification with Sam as mentor and father, we learn of Sam's own lineage. The story is a chilling one. Sam's father, the Indian Ikkemotubbe, is called *Du Homme* by a French traveling companion who likewise invents a titled name for himself. Ikkemotubbe corrupts *Du Homme* (which should properly have been *L'Homme*) into Doom. While the persistent examination of bloodlines and race in *Go Down, Moses* suggests that man is always his own fate—his own doom—Ikkemotubbe means to use the name as a way to intimidate others. But he does not rest on the resonant name alone. Rather, he runs away to exotic New Orleans, returning with fancy clothes, a quadroon slave (later Sam's mother), and a gold snuff-box filled with a mysterious white powder—which, he demonstrates, can instantly kill a young puppy. But if most of the Indians who observe this are fearful, the chief, Ikkemotubbe, is immune. So Doom sees that the chief's eight-year-old son and heir dies a similar death, and confirms his powers by demonstrating the powder's effect on yet another puppy, bringing about the resignation of Moketubbe and his own elevation to chief. The analogy Doom makes between the young boy and the young dogs may not come as a complete surprise after a similar analogy of persons with animals in "Was," but it is in a much darker vein.

Doom's inhumanity continues. He marries off to a black slave the quadroon he has impregnated, ridding himself of any responsibility for their liaison, and sells the couple to Lucius Quintus Carothers McCaslin. Doom's sense of possessing people and selling them to the family of "Was" thus retrospectively darkens "the old time, the old days" described there. We learn that the child born of mixed black, white, and Indian blood—Doom's child by a quadroon slave—is Sam Fathers. At sixty, squat and a bit flabby, he still displays physical signs of his ancestry. With hair as black and long as the mane of a horse, he is animallike, and thus not unlike those he kills in the Big Woods. His black ancestry is disclosed by "a slight dullness of the hair" and an expression in the eyes—"not the mark of servitude but of bondage"

(160–61). He not only resembles the quarry he hunts; he also displays an air of being trapped—"'Like an old lion or a bear in a cage,'" according to Cass (161). So Isaac or Cass, or both of them, are wrong on two counts, then, in their early impressions of Sam. There *is* a trace of negro in Sam's sense of bondage, and their easy allusion to animals suggests that Cass has remembered more from the days of "Was" than we might have suspected. Clearly, "the old time, the old days" are, for the McCaslins, centrally concerned with blacks, with slavery, and with race. The analogy does not seem to bother Isaac at this point, however; only the idea of a cage does. Isaac cries out to free Sam, and his cousin Cass only laughs (161).

The sound of Cass's laughter is important, although Isaac at once denies that is what it is. For the laughter suggests not only Cass's discrepant wisdom but also his despair. He understands well enough Sam's feelings and wishes to divorce himself from them: "'His cage aint us'" (162), he tells his cousin (and surrogate son) simply, directly. Strictly speaking, this is true; this is one mulatto on the McCaslin plantation for whom the McCaslins were not initially responsible. But they became responsible the moment L. Q. C. McCaslin paid Ikkemotubbe for Sam—and in that sense, Sam has brought the McCaslins into the cage with him.

What they cannot cage, however, is Sam's deep pride in being the son of a Chickasaw chief. In this sense, he refuses to be possessed, refuses to be caged, refuses to be a McCaslin despite their purchase of him, and he attempts to free himself from them by moving away from the cropland and the black quarters of the plantation to Jobaker's cabin in the Big Woods. He is still on McCaslin land, though, so he attempts to free himself further by making himself the mentor—and thus also the superior—of young Isaac. (He may not recognize his need to do this, but we do.) Yet Sam does not free himself entirely in the Big Woods, for he is never wholly Indian, and he is always partly McCaslin through purchase.

While Sam does not precisely possess the earth, as he would perhaps like to do, and while he teaches young Isaac the love and respect of nature, he nevertheless also uses nature to his own end. He kills to survive. He does not plant crops, as Cass does; he kills animals that run free near the riverbottom. The distinction may at first be a fine one that neither he nor Isaac sees, but it is insidious. What Sam is also implicitly teaching Isaac in teaching him the love and ways of the woods is to follow Sam in leaving behind the McCaslin plantation, with its hard work and unending responsibilities. Isaac is taking from Sam the pride of possessing the woods by possessing full knowledge of them, which Cass says, implicitly, are not Sam's (and surely not Isaac's) to possess.

In "The Old People," just as Sam is "himself his own battle-ground" (162) because he embodies disparate bloodlines, Isaac—now only a year older than Cass was in "Was"—is himself torn by conflicting loyalties to the disparate heritages represented by his two surrogate fathers. One, Sam, would hunt the land forever, as Uncle Buck had loved to do, and by way of ritual and the power of special knowledge (like Ikkemottube's special knowledge of the white powder?) thinks to make the land his. The other, Cass, would grow crops on the land to make it productive in a practical but less destructive, more honorable, and more responsible way.

The chapter ends with Cass attempting to drive home to Isaac the hard-won philosophy of the farmer, who finds his parable in the seeds that struggle to grow in the ground and bear fruit, and whose enemy is the carrion, or the world of nature that kills (179). As Cass presents this lesson to Isaac, the farmer's approach is a matter not of race or of ancestry but of perspective, a matter of position and responsibility; it is an alternative way of being in touch with the land, without selfishly using it or possessing it without claim or recompense. It is in that sense, too, that Cass attempts to instruct Isaac about the visionary buck that Sam addressed in Chickasaw, the magical language he shared with Jobaker but not with Isaac. Such wonderful visions as that, he says, are transcendent and inspirational, but have no substance and no shadow (180)—not because they do not occur, but because they take man away from the world at hand, where he is needed. What Cass means to do is to counter the frontier philosophy of Sam and of Uncle Buck with a plantation philosophy that will help Isaac carry forth the McCaslin name. He does not want Isaac to escape into the Big Woods, because if he were to do so, he would be surrendering all duty for a freedom that would, even on the surface, be self-indulgent. We cannot escape our cages, Cass insists, because we are our cages; DuHomme *is* Doom.

Thus, the note on which "The Old People" ends is both elegiac and melancholic. Cass knows that Isaac saw the mystical, visionary buck—so did he, once (180)—and that it is a vision the uninitiated, like the hunter Walter Ewell, are not privileged to see. But Cass's point is that even though he had had such an experience, his doom had been to return to the plantation. Visions come and go; hopes and dreams are fleeting, without substance or shadow. What is Sam's can never be Isaac's just as it could never be Cass's; it cannot be a part of the McCaslins, nor should it be. Race is indeed a cage, but not one from which a boy or man can courageously, willfully escape; race ineradicably shapes the conditions of one's life from birth. Ancestry is unrelinquishable. But the boy does not hear him, and Cass will not learn how deafened Isaac has become to that sense of reality until many years later, when the two of them discuss the McCaslin plantation ledgers they have jointly inherited, in part 4 of chapter 5, "The Bear."

The hunt for Old Ben in "The Bear" continues the paradox of the hunter as also the hunted until the demise of the Big Woods by the selling of the land to the lumber industry in 1883. The seduction of life in nature before the encroachment of civilization—whether railroad or plantation—is cause for some of Faulkner's most lyrical writing. Life in the woods each November is portrayed in sections 1 through 3 of "The Bear" as a life of Emersonian self-reliance, the sort of return to primitive nature praised by Thoreau, only now transferred to the riverbottoms of northern Mississippi: it is a "yearly pageant-rite" (186) involving "the best game of all" (184). But even such lyricism is hedged. Each section of "The Bear" detailing the hunt for Old Ben begins with an ominous warning: "There was a man and a dog too this time" (183); "So he should have hated and feared Lion" (201); "It was December. It was the coldest December he had ever remembered" (217). These opening lines function as slight tremors of matters about to go awry.

Yet while the hunters' quarry may seem monumental, immortal, and visionary in certain passages of the story, Faulkner's first description of Old Ben reveals that he is an aging animal with a maimed foot;

a legendary killer of young shoats and grown pigs, a mangler of dogs; a beast that has left "a corridor of wreckage and destruction" but remains himself indestructible (185). Ike would be awestruck by him; hunters would use him as a totem for their ritual game each fall; but to the ordinary people, to the swampers and townsfolk who appear in sections 2 and 3, who come sensing Ben's death, he is ruinous and murderous of life and property.

Ike, however, imbued with Sam's sense of the sacredness of the totemic animal, can no more see Ben's harmful and evil ways than he can understand Cass's pleas for responsibility and agrarianism. In the course of Faulkner's narrative, the bear makes eight epiphanic appearances to Ike, each time drawing the boy closer to its own mystique of dominance (which makes Old Ben, like Sam, a kind of father, although a childless bachelor). Increasingly, Ike yearns to see Ben up close, to establish the bear's special quality, and to form his own special relationship with the bear, as Sam has. On his third attempt, leaving behind the gun that might kill Ben and then, in turn, the compass and watch that mark Ike as a member of civilization rather than of Ben's world of nature, Ike is finally rewarded with the mystical vision he seeks (200–201). But in this manifestation, Ben's appearance is, tellingly, like that of the great buck in "The Old People," which Cass tries to explain away. Like the buck, Old Ben is suddenly before Ike and then, just as suddenly, irrevocably fades away. Like the buck, the bear is without substance and shadow.

But Old Ben, unlike the buck, is huge and dominant, proud and self-contained, dimensionless, with no clear size or shape. His return into the primordial darkness, where he has learned, we must assume, his ways of ravaging the other life of the countryside—invading farms and livestock to keep its wilderness pure and its own—is a symbolic warning. Like Ikkemotubbe, Old Ben is despotic. More important, Old Ben reveals to us (although not to Ike) the futility of the boy's relinquishing his gun, watch, and compass: the bear leaves those talismans of civilization for Ike, who returns to them, ready to take up the hunt that Ben has continued to allow—indeed, has all but reinstituted. Cass has repeatedly told Ike that fundamental conditions do not change; now Ben proves it.

Ike does not really comprehend Old Ben or his significance; he merely witnesses him. But Ike hears and acknowledges. Sam, who teaches the boy to temper his pride in the woods with humility before them—a humility that nonetheless facilitates and permits killing, in time and over time. Sam teaches Ike not to be fearful, since animals can sense fear in their contest with men, but to be scared, since that is a warning condition natural to the hunter (198). In this, Ike proves to be a good pupil. What Ike does not learn, but what becomes clear to Sam the moment he finds the mutilated corpse of a three-month-old colt (205), is that death and destruction can breed only death and destruction. Sam's life has been one of teaching young Ike how to hunt rather than how to preserve, and now Sam's time, like Ben's, has run out: he sees his own life as finally emptying out and empty. He is childless, the end of his line, a model for Ike, to which Ike will remain blind (206).

At least Sam recognizes the significance of Ikkemotubbe/Doom: his fate, his doom, is to be black. At 70, Sam is still confined, caged by his black blood (206). Thus, Sam is especially drawn to his mirror image in the dog Lion, that wholly malevolent beast that knows only killing, that is nearly mechanical (gunlike) in his desire to maim, mutilate, and destroy, like Old Ben (209). Sam's fascination with Lion, his need to capture and cage him, and his sheer focused energy in starving him into obedience—something which, pointedly, so fascinates Ike that he asks to stay on a few days longer to observe Sam, himself in the process of dying, establishing dominance over the dog—is telling.

The boy also fails to see, in Boon Hogganbeck's love of and need for whiskey, that the behavior of this part-Indian resembles the behavior displayed long ago (in "Was") by Ike's father, Uncle Buck. Boon's drinking is caused by his prescience of death, which he shares with Sam but not with Ike.

When the death of Old Ben comes, it comes at a cost: the death of Lion, the eventual death of Sam, and the sanity of Boon. That is the actuality; these are the facts. But Faulkner describes the killing of Ben in terms that evoke a beautiful ballet. Boon, attempting to save Lion from Ben's attack, "leap[s] among the hounds . . . and fling[s] himself astride the bear" from behind. Locking his legs around Ben's belly and pulling back against the bear's throat with one arm, Boon then plunges his knife into Ben's body to secure his death. "For an instant," dog, bear, and man "almost resemble a piece of statuary" (230–31). The event is forced into this description as a ballet because it reminds Ike, in its details, of the way in which Sam had taught him to kill the buck when he was only 12. Ike sees Boon's actions as a way to avoid a gun in a heroic effort to kill Old Ben in order to save Lion—but the language used to describe those actions does not match Ike's perception. The language grows out of Boon's bizarre love of the malevolent dog, and the "loverlike" grip in which Ben holds Lion is what finally prompts Boon to race into battle with Old Ben. Boon's initial position "astride" the bear—followed by his penetration of Old Ben with his knife—is quickly regained after they fall together. Clearly, what Faulkner is indicating is an act of rape on Boon's part, stemming from the bear's embrace of Lion—but that rape also serves as a metaphor for the rape of the woods, the rape of the hunters, the rape of civilization attempting to interrupt the ways of nature. It is unnecessary intervention, savage and selfish. Hunted and hunter merge in an unending—but destructive—contest for dominance. In fact, the attention of the hunters is wholly on their quarry, on the wounded Ben and the wounded Lion. It is only the black McCaslin, Tennie's Jim Beauchamp, whose vision is larger: he notices that Sam Fathers is lying face-down in the mud (231).

The death of Old Ben is followed shortly by the deaths of Lion and of Sam. But all three chapters of ritual hunts have occurred during a period of incalculable loss and death, with the hunting and killing of rabbit, deer, and bear standing in for and distracting attention from the real tragedies that have occurred in the world outside the hunts for Tomey's Turl and the game of the forest. From 1859 to 1883 the entire Confederate South has been defeated by Union forces that killed unprecedented numbers of men on both sides; during this period, Warwick has burnt to the ground, and Hubert has sought refuge on the McCaslin plantation. There have been a large number of personal deaths too: all three of Tomey's Turl's and Tennie's newborn infants, Uncle Buck, Uncle Buddy, Sophonsiba, Hubert, Jobaker. The death knell has rung repeatedly on the McCaslin plantation, and Cass has carried the burden of that knowledge to Isaac in each of the hunting stories. Now, after the conclusion of the contest to kill Old Ben, Sam is dying, and it is time for Cass to take Isaac back to the plantation. But Isaac refuses to go (239). General Compson intervenes on Isaac's behalf, because he thinks the boy needs time in the woods to come to terms with the changes, and because he believes that as a good woodsman, Isaac belongs there.

Although Isaac insists that he has to stay, he will not tell the hunters why (240). If we do not surmise his reason at first, Faulkner soon reveals the woodland practice to which the part-Indian Boon is privy: the need to help Sam Fathers die and to bury him. As Isaac has been trained in the woods to bring about the end of life in the woods, it is only natural for him to want to continue to participate in what Boon knows and what Sam would want.

When Cass returns on the following Sunday morning to fetch Isaac, as they have agreed, he already finds Boon estranged, maddened by the events, protecting Sam. Cass asks Boon if he is responsible for Sam's burial, but Boon denies that he had a part in the man's death. The scene is an uncanny repetition of the scene that closed "The Old People," and Cass uses the same method with Boon that he had tried without success on Isaac. In "The Old People," Cass said he had seen the special vision of the deer that Isaac thought he alone had been privileged to see. Now Cass says he would shoot Sam, as Boon feels singularly privileged to do—and he says it for the same reason. He wants to force on Boon—and on Isaac, who protests such treatment by Cass—the truth, the actuality of what they have done. He is not judging their right to do it or even the morality of their act; he is forcing them to take the responsibility for what they freely chose to do. He means to show them the dimensions (and limits) of their freedom to choose, within the bondage of their lives, within the rough edges of their doom. He wants to teach them wider lessons about life and death.

But the chasm between them is already much too wide. The plantation realities that Sophonsiba knew and that Cass (rather than Sophonsiba's own son, Isaac) has inherited still cannot speak directly to the frontiersmen and hunters who would live out their lives free of the past. Later in *Go Down, Moses*, Faulkner argues more openly that no one can escape his past, any more than he can escape his caste, class, race, or genealogy. The inescapable burden of history and its sometimes unbearable weight are what a sense of chronology always makes clear. We can no more escape time as process and force than Cass can. Those who ignore reality—the reality of the world around them, of death and dying, of the ineradicable conditions of the past—are doomed. Even in "the old times, the old days," such matters have unavoidably intervened and changed them all forever.

6

Then
(1884–1921)

Romance and controversy seemed to stalk and haunt Section
Thirteen. A contemporary of William McKendree Gwin was William
Pinchback, a man who left a line as distinguished as his neighbor. A
line drawn across racial proscriptions that remains in the memory
and dower of Providence and Township Sixteen. An identifiable
community and lake still bear his name nearby. Pinchback owned
Section Eleven, a part of what was later to be Providence Plantation.

Like Gwin, Pinchback was the owner of much land and many
slaves. Toward the end of his life he executed a remarkable contract
with one of his neighbors. He sold him five slaves for a hundred dollars. The market price would have been a thousand dollars apiece.
The document stipulated "at some appropriate time or at the request
of said slaves they are to be taken to one of the new slave states and
there set free." Perhaps knowing he would not live much longer or
perhaps feeling the hot breath of war that was already blowing across
the Cotton Kingdom in the late 1840s, Major Pinchback had already
accomplished what he called upon his neighbor to do in this document. He had taken Eliza Stewart, a slave woman, and the children
she had borne him to Philadelphia where they were legally manumit-
ted. They came to his plantation in Holmes County where they lived
in peace. Perhaps he had executed the second document as further

insurance that the woman he loved and their children would not be reenslaved in Mississippi upon his death.

When William Pinchback died, his executor immediately sent Eliza Stewart and her children to Cincinnati so white relatives could not disinherit and reenslave them. He failed in his first endeavor but succeeded in the second. The family of Major William Pinchback was denied their inheritance but remained free. But freedom in poverty.

A respectable and successful planter could alter bloodlines with impunity in the nineteenth century, with no recriminations nor expulsion from the community because of his interracial family. A hundred years later, issue of those tolerant neighbors would drive from camp a little band of Christian missionaries whose offense was civility to the fruit of Eliza Stewart's womb. (Campbell, 92–93)

The ledgers housed in the McCaslin plantation commissary, which stretch backward to the earliest known written statements of the family and forward to anticipate its decline in the lives of Ike and Roth—all the family accounts receivable—form the narrative spine of *Go Down, Moses* and serve as the focal point of the second main chronological period, 1884–1921, when the family lands are under the management of Zack and Cass. Two major episodes in the novel take place during that period. One is chronicled in sections 4 and 5 of chapter 5, "The Bear," the other in the third part of chapter 2, "The Fire and the Hearth." Together, they make explicit family events that result from the miscegenation that produced the McCaslin and Beauchamp relationship.

As "Was" moves somewhere between the tall tale and the serious problem of the runaway slave, so these episodes of plantation life move between the sentimental plantation novel, which serves Faulkner as the antitype of *Go Down, Moses*, and the realistic novel of slave rebellion. Both may be found, in different degrees, in John Pendleton Kennedy's *Swallow Barn* (1832), which Michael Grimwood has called the prototype of the romantic plantation novel picturing the South in the nineteenth century.[43] In depicting the Meriwether plantation, Swallow Barn, and the neighboring Tracy plantation, The Brakes, through a series of nearly discrete episodes, the book distantly resembles *Go Down, Moses*, in which the McCaslin plantation borders on that of the Beauchamp family. Kennedy takes pains to disregard and

Greenfield Farm, Faulkner's model for the McCaslin commissary and plantation. *Photograph by Arthur F. Kinney.*

thus dismiss any disagreeable features of plantation life that do not imitate the life of the landed gentry of England, much as Sophonsiba does in naming the Beauchamp plantation Warwick. Until very near the end of his widely popular novel, Kennedy avoids any indication of racial tension, providing instead an ideal conception of plantation life as the American version of the earlier ideal English pastoral.

As Kennedy began his final draft of *Swallow Barn* in September 1830, he added some new material; the next year, while he was revising it, Nat Turner led an insurrection of blacks against their white owners and, as a kind of Moses, promised to deliver them from bondage. The rebellion shocked the nation, and especially the South, as Turner and his followers killed more than fifty whites. That Kennedy thought this important but difficult to confront seems clear, because he moved the setting of his novel, for no known reason, to within 50 miles of the Turner uprising in Southampton, Virginia. Clearly, for Kennedy, the ideals of plantation life were both antidote and protective shield against the realities of black-white relations on Southern plantations. It is just this that may have helped, in some early way, to suggest to Faulkner the contours of *Go Down, Moses*—although other plantation novels, following the pioneering effort of Kennedy, doubtless had their influence too, both on Faulkner and on Faulkner's early readers. The desire of the older white generation in *Swallow Barn* to keep blacks in their place is the driving force reflected by the commissary records on the McCaslin plantation.

In the correlative episodes in "The Fire and the Hearth," racial tensions break out openly in Lucas Beauchamp's irrational but undeniable conviction that to take vengeance on Zack Edmonds is the only way to maintain his honor, his manliness. When writing those episodes, Faulkner may have had in the recesses of his mind a historical event that was as well known as the uprising of Nat Turner, and surely as celebrated: the murder in 1819 of Colonel Solomon P. Sharp, a prominent lawyer and political figure in Frankfort, Kentucky, by Jereboam Beauchamp. The crime led to the publication of Beauchamp's confession as an "autobiography" and inspired popular ballads, a play by Edgar Allan Poe, and fiction by William Gilmore Simms and Robert Penn Warren.[44] There was no racial strife between the two men—both were white—but there was an assault on honor: Beauchamp's wife gave birth, she said, to Sharp's bastard child, and Sharp, to save himself during a political campaign, called the child a mulatto (and therefore surely not his). This led to Beauchamp's attempt to fight Sharp in a fair duel, but Sharp (like Zack) refused. Unlike the fictional conflict between Zack and Lucas, which ends in an uneasy truce, the real-life conflict ended with Beauchamp killing Sharp. Later, both he and his wife attempted suicide. She was successful, he was not, and was publicly hanged for murder.

Whether or not Faulkner was thinking of the Sharp murder, the Turner uprising, or both while he was composing *Go Down, Moses* (both were doubtless known to him), those incidents are instructive because they illustrate the realistic and romantic perspectives that keep the fictional cousins Cass and Ike forever beyond full communication, full communal brotherhood. This fundamental division of attitudes, at the heart and center of *Go Down, Moses*, begins in section 4 of "The Bear," wherein Ike makes two visits to the commissary (in 1884 and again in 1888) to address his genealogy and his inheritance in the family ledgers.

The building's walls are covered with old advertisements for various goods and luxuries "sold by white men to . . . negroes that they might resemble the very race" that had controlled them for so long; old smells of cheese and leather permeate the air (244). Ignoring the set of ledgers recording "the slow outward trickle of food and supplies and equipment which returned each fall as cotton made and ginned and sold," Ike goes straight to the "clumsy and archaic" older ledgers with their yellowing pages. In these books his father, Theophilus (Uncle Buck), and his uncle, Amodeus (Uncle Buddy), recorded their own personal version of the manumission of the slaves they inherited from L. Q. C. McCaslin in the two decades before the Civil War (245). Here is written testimony concerning the family's identity, history, and legacy—a faded record of transactions that documents family actions and attempts to justify them. For Ike, however, the ledgers also constitute a new hunting ground. The death of Old Ben has emptied the wilderness of any significance for him—but the ledgers quite possibly contain information about Sam Fathers, who was for much of his life a McCaslin slave, and whose death Ike has just witnessed. Here, Faulkner skillfully conveys meaning through analogy and juxtaposition: The arc Ike travels through the pages of the past follows, with uncanny resonance, his recent experiences in the Big Woods. His responses, too, move from an initial wonderment and attraction to a sense of darkening tragedy and, finally, to a recognition of doom harbored in and yet somehow beyond both the woods and all mortality.

Ike cannot remember a time when these ledgers were not present for him. When he was a child of 9 or 10 or 11, although they seemed strange and talismanic to him, he had no desire to read them (256). But since the death of Sam, his surrogate father (despite Sam's mixed genealogy), who was also a McCaslin slave (and so a part of these books), they are no longer "harmless" (256). Indeed, the 16-year-old Ike now approaches these ledgers with a furtive urgency. After midnight, he goes into Cass's room to get the key to the commissary while his cousin is sleeping, and then proceeds quietly to the commissary, where he locks the door behind him (257). While it is true that any information the ledgers contain is necessarily open to Ike's interpretation—that he reads in them not a financial account but his own narrative of the family's history and of its racial past, subject to his and his culture's imagination—he comes to find what he knows he will find in his deepest and darkest but surest premonitions (256; 256–57). Later memories will temper his initial dread with the humorous entries regarding the slave Percival Brownlee, bought from Nathan Bedford Forrest at Cold Water on March 3, 1856, for $265. The running account of the hapless Brownlee (252–54) provides some distraction from the earliest entries, which at first raise troubling questions in Ike's mind and later take on far more significance.

These entries tell of Ike's grandfather, L. Q. C. McCaslin, who was born in Carolina in 1772 and died in Mississippi on June 27, 1837; of the slave Roskus, raised by old Carothers's father, who was freed the day Carothers died, but who did not want to leave the plantation; of Roskus's wife, Fibby, who was freed the same day but also refused to leave; and of their son, Thucydus, born in Carolina in 1779 who *"Refused 10acre peace fathers Will 28 Jun 1837 Refused Cash offer $200. dolars from A. @ T. McCaslin 28 Jun 1837 Wants to stay and work it out"* (254–55).

We can reconstruct Ike's reading of the ledgers because he is selective; these entries are important to his needs and to his understanding. He skims the next five pages (255) to follow the fate of Thucydus, on whom he has become fixated by the previous entries.

Soon he finds the final entry—a double notation written by his father, Uncle Buck. The first part reads, "*3 Nov 1841 By Cash to Thucydus McCaslin $200. dolars Set Up blaksmith in J. Dec 1841 Dide and burid in J. 17 feb 1854*" (255). The second part, apparently an independent notation, reads, "*Eunice Bouth by Father in New Orleans 1807 $650. dolars. Marrid to Thucydus 1809 Drownd in Crick Cristmas Day 1832*" (255). Apparently, Uncle Buck had connected these two events, because the dates (1854 and 1832) indicate that these notations otherwise would have been entered chronologically and thus would have been separated by a number of pages. It is as if the death of Thucydus not only reminded him of the death of Thucydus's wife, Eunice, but also freed him to enter her death and its extraordinary cause, drowning, on Christmas Day—an unlikely date for such a death, not least because the ice would have made an accidental drowning difficult and improbable.

Evidently, Uncle Buck's notation of Eunice's death opens wounds: Uncle Buddy feels forced to correct the entry (something Ike sees nowhere else in the ledgers) by writing beneath it, "Drownd herself." Uncle Buck denies this in a subsequent entry expressing his belief that no blacks commit suicide—but Uncle Buddy defiantly insists by again writing "Drownd herself," and Ike is left puzzled (256). But he is then only 16.

When Ike returns to the ledgers in 1884, it is this riddle he means to resolve. How did his uncle know the drowning was suicide, and why did he insist that the fact be recorded in the plantation account books? Again, he has a premonition of what he will find out by reading more in the ledgers. The two entries that come hard on the heels of the delayed announcements of Eunice's death—although they contain information Ike already knows—confirm his premonition. The first reads, "*Tomasina called Tomy Daughter of Thucydus @ Eunice Born 1810 dide in Child bed June 1833 and Burd. Yr stars fell*"; the next, "*Turl Son of Thucydus @ Eunice Tomy born Jun 1833 yrs stars fell Fathers will*" (257).

Eunice's death is thus somehow connected in Uncle Buck's and Uncle Buddy's minds with their half-brother, Tomey's Turl—and "*Fathers will*" suggests that although L. Q. C. McCaslin, at least, did not acknowledge his paternity, he provided for his bastard son in his will. This confirms for Ike what he already knows: that old Carothers left a thousand-dollar legacy to Tomey's Turl because he had fathered the boy by his own slave, Tomasina. The fact is an ugly one, if not historically uncommon—and Ike's grandfather had admitted his own child (as Colonel W. C. Falkner had admitted his) only through his legacy. Yet even in this distant way, Carothers showed more concern for his son than Ikkemotubbe showed for Sam.

For Ike, there are still unanswered questions. His hunting, racing imagination continues to probe the riddles in the McCaslin past. Why, for instance, had old Carothers, who "never went anywhere" and who surely needed no more slaves, gone to New Orleans and bought Eunice (258–59)? In pondering a possible explanation, Ike almost begins to think his grandfather purchased Eunice as "a wife for Thucydus," but he stops himself—because suddenly looming stranger and more important than the slaves' marriage was old Carothers's extraordinary trip to New Orleans, which in no way fit his usual pattern of behavior, to secure that marriage. Why would he suddenly go so far? Why New Orleans? How would he know what he might find there? Apparently, he had never been to New Orleans before, for there is no mention of it elsewhere in the ledgers. The only answer possible is that Carothers had known Eunice before he bought her. So there was love, after all—although it appears that old McCaslin's love eventually went to Tomasina.

The ledger pages, which now seem to turn themselves before Ike's very eyes (259), return him to the original entry regarding the purchase of Eunice by his grandfather. She was bought in New Orleans in 1807 for $650—substantially more than the $265 he paid, years later, for the male slave Brownlee. Eunice's price supports Ike's apparent new contention that his grandfather knew Eunice and thought of her as someone special—and two neighboring entries on Thucydus, to whom she was married in 1809, suggest more. The first of these, written by Uncle Buck, indicates that Thucydus *"Refused 10acre peace fathers Will 28 Jun 1837"* and *"Refused Cash offer $200. dolars from A. @ T. McCaslin 28 Jun 1837 Wants to stay and work it out"* (254–55). Clearly, in his first reading of the ledgers, Ike had thought, innocently enough, that his father and uncle were granting old Thucydus freedom. But why should his grandfather's will, which left a legacy to Tomey's Turl as his offspring, have also left a legacy of ten acres of land (which Uncle Buck may have subconsciously interpreted as a peace offering, hence his misspelling) to a man born in 1779 and unrelated to him? What debt was his grandfather attempting to pay off? Put another way, what guilt was old Carothers attempting to assuage, and what responsibility was he actually acknowledging? The second entry on Thucydus reveals that at the age of 62—four years after his refusal of the land and the offer of cash—he finally accepted a payment of $200 and left the plantation permanently, as a free man, to set up his own blacksmith shop in Jefferson where he died and was buried in 1854 (255).

The entry regarding Carothers's purchase of Eunice in 1807 also notes that she was married to Thucydus in 1809. If Eunice was bought to be Thucydus's wife, why were they not married until two years later? And why did Eunice commit suicide when her daughter, Tomasina, was pregnant 23 years later? Something about Tomasina— born in 1810, within months of her marriage to Thucydus—must have been a factor. For Ike, the only way to make sense of these records is to assume that Carothers had impregnated Eunice with Tomasina and covered his misdeed by marrying her to Thucydus (just as Ikkemotubbe had married off his mistress, a quadroon slave, when he impregnated her with Sam). To ease his conscience, Carothers left a peace offering of 10 acres of land to Thucydus in his will. But the gesture did not work: Thucydus, who had some dignity of his own, some loyalty to his wife, and perhaps some loyalty to his foster child, refused the property. (Ike does not stop to imagine the quiet rage Thucydus must have felt throughout the years as a powerless witness to Carothers's actions and their consequences.) Both Ike's father and Uncle Buddy must have known the reasons behind their father's bequest to Thucydus, because when he rejected it, they offered him a cash settlement instead.

Ike now realizes that Tomasina's son, Tomey's Turl—the quarry in Cass's story about the hunt and the poker game, who in 1884 is living with Ike on the McCaslin plantation (he will die in 1887)—is not only Uncle Buck's and Uncle Buddy's half-brother; Tomey's Turl is also the grandson of his own father, old Carothers, who sired Tomasina. Knowing that, Ike knows all he wants to know: "that was all. He would never need look at the ledgers again nor did he" (259). Ike's ancestors, then—the predecessors who would serve him as models—are whites who invade and impregnate blacks, commit incest, and try to buy off their guilt and shame, and blacks who struggle to maintain their dignity and, when that fails, repudiate their family, even at the cost of life, to preserve honor.

The following year—whether to test his own bondage to his family's past or to test his own possibility of relinquishing it—Ike returns to the land of his childhood, to the Big Woods, where the lumber company is now cutting timber (301). At first, General Compson and Walter Ewell had attempted to decrease their loss by incorporating themselves into a hunting club that could lease the camp and woods, but a short time later Major de Spain sells the timber rights to a lumber company in Memphis—repeating Ikkemotubbe's original sin against the land. Ike knew this much before he returned to the woods; he should have suspected more, and perhaps he did.

In 1883, on the day of Old Ben's death, Ike had recalled watching the bear's "thick, locomotive-like shape" crash through the woods four years earlier (228); now, in 1885, Ike is riding a train into those same woods, and from its cupola he can see part of the train ahead of him, curving snakelike before disappearing from view. Once he arrives at the old hunting land, nothing seems right. He is met by Ash, who tells him that Boon is outside the woods, shooting at squirrels in a sweet-gum tree and expecting Ike to join him. Yet Ash insists that he will serve Boon and Ike dinner within the hour, before 10 in the morning, or not at all (308). After a futile attempt to persuade Ash to make dinner later, Ike heads off to find Boon.

As he walks in solitude through the woods, Ike recalls that years ago—the day after he had killed his first buck—Ash, who knew nothing about hunting, set out with the boy to kill a deer himself, but only ended up ineptly trying to shoot a yearling bear they encountered. During their foray into the woods, Ash kept up "an old man's garrulous monologue," including a boastful comment on his adulterous thoughts about "a new light-colored woman who nursed next door to Major de Spain's" (310).

Ike's reverie about Ash's incompetence in the woods and thoughts of adultery ends when he arrives at the forest plot where Sam Fathers and Lion are buried. The graves are already beginning to disappear, as the footprints of Old Ben had years ago (312, 200). On the ground above the dog's grave, beneath the leaves, Ike finds the metal box containing Ben's paw. The man-made tin that once held grease for man-made engines has outlasted the cycles of nature, about which Sam had taught him; it has not deteriorated in the way that Old Ben's maimed foot and Lion's bleached bones have decayed. Back in the sunlight, Ike remembers that earlier, Ash had warned him, "[W]atch your feet. They're crawling" (308)—and at that moment he sees the snake, now inversely recalling the locomotive (314). The deer of old is replaced by the snake of the present, and Ike, deliberately echoing Sam in his address to it, seals the analogy: " 'Chief,' he said: 'Grandfather' " (314).

Ike becomes aware of a persistent sound. Approaching it, he realizes that it is coming from the vicinity of the gum tree, where he finds Boon hammering his gun barrel against the breach "with the frantic abandon of a madman" (315). Boon does not welcome Ike back to the woods but forces him away, claiming sole possession of all the squirrels in the tree. Not like his white predecessors, then, but like his black ones, Ike is dispossessed—if possession were ever even possible.

Boon, victimized by his mixed blood as Sam was forever caged by his, has turned to their shared belief in the purity of nature, only to find that if it had uncontaminated origins, they were origins he would never know—origins lost now in a mythical Edenic past, past snakes and locomotives, lumber companies and maddened squirrels. But if such a myth is no longer available to Boon or to Ike in the summer of 1885, Ike can at least return to the ledgers he finally deciphered in the winter of 1884. Unable to achieve innocence again in the Big Woods, he can take up his family's unfulfilled responsibilities by supplying to James (Tennie's Jim) and Sophonsiba (Fonsiba) Beauchamp their rightful legacy—now $1,000 each because his father and uncle had tripled Carothers's unpaid legacy, only to leave that too unpaid.

Ike may recall that the ledger entry for James, half-nephew to his father and uncle, shows he was nearly named for them—first for Theophilus and then for Amodeus—as if to atone for past wrongs (260–61). But his trip is futile; he is unable to find his cousin and returns to the plantation commissary to enter his failure in the historical record of the ledgers himself—himself now becoming a part of them, a part of the family, relinquishing the Big Woods and surrendering the possibility of ever paying Tennie's Jim, the friend who had first called attention to the fallen Sam Fathers the day Old Ben and Lion were killed (261).

Then there is Fonsiba. In the ledgers Uncle Buck so abbreviates Fonsiba's birth that he nearly erases all connection with it—"*Miss sophonsiba b drt t t @ t 1869*" (262)—even though his black half-niece is given his own wife's name. This reluctant sense of involvement may inspire Fonsiba's own rebelliousness (or her sense of not being wanted at all), for in 1886, at the age of 17, she announces in the McCaslin commissary her intention to marry a man from the North. The shock to Cass, which Ike observes, leads to a conversation that, consciously or not, Ike will repeat decades later with the granddaughter of Tennie's Jim, her brother (in chapter 6, "Delta Autumn"). Ike listens to the words exchanged by Cass and the man Fonsiba will marry with mounting incredulity.

> "[Y]our father was a slave."
> "Yes. Once."
> "Then how do you own a farm in Arkansas?"
> "I have a grant. It was my father's. From the Unites States. For military service."
> "I see," McCaslin said. "The Yankee army."
> "The United States army," the stranger said. (263)

Cass has as little love for this son of a black Union soldier who will take Fonsiba off to a carpetbagger's farm as Ike will have for the granddaughter of Tennie's Jim—and, presaging Ike's future behavior, Cass does not even ask the man his name. Instead, his judgment and his dismissal (like Ike's later) is abrupt, stern, and final: "'Go'" (264). And, as the granddaughter of Tennie's Jim will in "Delta Autumn," the unnamed black displays the humanity that Fonsiba's father, Tomey's

Turl, had attempted to teach Uncle Buck and Uncle Buddy so long ago: "'Be easy. I will be good to her'" (264).

Five months later, in late 1886, Ike travels to Arkansas to deliver Fonsiba's legacy to her, just as he had traveled, a year earlier, in an unsuccessful attempt to find Tennie's Jim for the same reason. The journey is an arduous one. He goes by rail, stage, hired livery, and rail again. He sleeps in hotels, roadside taverns, strangers' cabins, and haylofts (265). In his strong need to find her, he empowers himself to succeed by fantasizing that he is one of the Magi, journeying anonymously—his own myth of origin.

What he finds, on unfarmed land, is a shack in which Fonsiba crouches behind a table, clearly fearful of her own white relative. In the next room, her husband sits "in the only chair in the house," dressed in the black clothes of a clergyman, reading a book through spectacles with no lenses (266). But he retains his dignity and independence and refuses Ike's money. Thunderstruck, humiliated, anxious—having already failed as Moses, hoping to redeem James; now having failed as one of the Magi, bearing his gift of gold to Fonsiba; failing even as a member of the white South, yearning to breathe free—Ike now sees not just his own family but also the entire South and all its inhabitants, black and white, cursed by the history permanently inked in the ledgers in the McCaslin commissary. His straightforward catechism to Fonsiba's husband about the curse whites have brought on the land (266) shows the pride Sam has taught Ike, but not humility: it displays, in its insidious way, Carothers McCaslin's own attitude of taking up responsibility after asking that others do so.

The man with the vision—and the humanity still—is the Yankee black who says, and Fonsiba will agree, that what matters is their freedom, and they now have that. Freed from slavery means, for them, freed from McCaslins. Ike thus learns from the blacks in his family, who really want nothing to do with him, what Uncle Buck and Uncle Buddy and the proud Sam Fathers and the maddened Boon Hogganbeck did not learn—but what Cass tried to teach Ike, even in the woods: one cannot evade responsibility for the past nor erase it; one cannot simply atone for it, pay it off with increased cash. One has, instead, to learn to live with it.

We can measure how far Faulkner himself has come, as a descendant of the South, by comparing this unnamed black in "The Bear" with the unnamed black who is the protagonist of his early story "Sunset," first published in the New Orleans *Times-Picayune* on 24 May 1925[45] and included in *William Faulkner: New Orleans Sketches*. That black, while sympathetically portrayed, is untutored and ignorant. He wants only to return to Africa, but the senseless impossibility of his plans causes him to be the butt of jokes and tricks. A white steamboat captain takes all his money, promising to transport him to Africa (*Sketches*, 80). For this, he is required to help other blacks shift cargo before his is put ashore. In the darkness, he shoots a cow in fright, certain it is a lion about to take his life. Set upon by an armed white group defending the public safety, he is wounded by a pistol, kills in response, escapes to a thicket, kills again, and is finally, while delirious, killed himself (*Sketches*, 85). In contrast to this homeless outsider seeking Africa, Fonsiba's husband—despite his lenseless glasses (or perhaps because of them)—sees deeply into the tragedy of American history and confronts, with mature judgment, the cost of that past and the consequences he must deal with and live through. And so does Fonsiba; she knows that with him—but not on the McCaslin plantation—she is free.

In 1888 Ike turns 21. He has long since absorbed the lesson of Percival Brownlee, the bookkeeper-revivalist-brothel proprietor freed in 1856 (252–53, 279–80); he has learned that his father's equating of animals and blacks ("*1 Oct 1856 Mule josephine Broke Leg @ shot Wrong stall wrong niger wrong everything $100. dolars*" [253]) continued long after the hunt for Tomey's Turl. He has long known about his father's and uncle's ambivalent and inadequate response to slavery itself—nightly "locking" the McCaslin slaves into the plantation house, "which lacked half its windows and had no hinged back door at all," so that they were at liberty to skulk along the roads at night, dodging Patrol-riders (251). But Ike has displaced all this with the knowledge of the biblical land of Canaan and the understanding of relinquishment he has learned in attempting to pay off his black relatives, James and Fonsiba Beauchamp.

Facing Cass once more in the commissary, Ike surprises his cousin by declaring that he will relinquish all rights and responsibilities to the McCaslin land (245). To Cass, it is a brutal remark. All his life, he has meant to teach Ike responsibility for his actions in the real world in which he lives. Now Ike, unable to bear the burden of McCaslin history, having tried unsuccessfully to pay off its debts, wants to be rid of it entirely and forever. He has found a way to make sense of this, too, by combining Sam's worship of the land with Fonsiba's husband's sense of the curse. He argues that man never owned the land to begin with—that he was placed on earth by God merely to be an overseer. But in attempting to assert ownership of the earth—in declaring it his, as God declared all creation His—man has blasphemed and has dispossessed himself not only of the right to buy and sell land but also of the right to buy and sell those who would work on it (246–47).

Ike is obsessed with his own guilt and unsubscribed involvement through inheritance; having failed as Moses and as one of the Magi, he will sacrifice his legacy. Why else was he named Isaac (248, 270–71)? If he cannot pay off the black McCaslins to relieve himself of the shame and guilt of his miscegenetic and even incestuous ancestry, then he will, like them, lift the curse by voiding the past. The hubris here is stunning, and it stuns Cass—but it absolutely blinds Ike. For only by the strangest and most irrational twistings of his sources (Genesis 12–25, I Chronicles 1:32) can Ike lay claim to any biblical precedent in sacrificing his own responsibilities for his family's plantation and his own responsibility for paternity by both repudiating and relinquishing his birthright (surely, one act would cancel out the other) and by transferring his obligations to a cousin on the distaff side of his family line, who has all along accepted them. The biblical Isaac had twins, Esau and Jacob, rather than being born *of* a twin, and it was not Isaac but his son Esau—a cunning hunter and man of the field—who bargained away his inheritance.

Clearly, Faulkner's point—if not Ike's—is that Ike's very attempt to rationalize his selfish bid for release from the past when he confronts Cass is an indication that Ike, like his grandfather and father before him, is attempting to formulate an action that will free him from the bondage of his past and of his family's past actions. The explicit and implicit narrative by which Ike sets *himself* free emulates and mocks God's own sacred history and suggests that the role of Isaac—to perform a sacrifice—is no truer to Ike's condition and no more within his grasp than his previously assumed biblical roles. The sheer audacity of his proposal—and his fierce blindness to his own past acts—demonstrates the extent of his arrogance and pride.

But in time, even Ike is not convinced of this line of argument, and he tries once more, obsessively, unstoppable, in the novel's longest monologue (271–81), to trace once more the history of the Western world and his place in it. The intricate pressures of the past culture alongside the past behavior of the McCaslin family must, at any cost, be clarified—and this time, through history, Ike finds that the answers lie not with him or with Cass but with the blacks. Their endurance alone will save both blacks and whites.

As so often before—back in the woods, here in the commissary—Cass tries to break through Ike's fabling, his narrating, his role-playing. Seeing that pointing out individual exceptions will do no good, he mocks Ike by opposing Ike's generalities with equally specious ones of his own. He opposes the grand virtues Ike assigns to all blacks with equally potent vices: "'Promiscuity. Violence. Instability and lack of control'" (281). When Ike points out that blacks have fidelity, Cass's reply is "'So have dogs'" (282). For Cass can no more tolerate Ike's excessive patronizing of blacks than he can tolerate Ike's own self-patronizing.

As if to prove Cass's position, the two of them return to their house to complete their celebration of Ike's twenty-first birthday by opening his long-held legacy from Hubert—that is, not the McCaslin legacy, but the Beauchamp one. What they find instead of the expected "silver cup filled with gold pieces" (287), however, is an "unstained tin coffee-pot" containing a handful of copper coins and stacks of I.O.U. notes (292–93) (which, in their formulaic language, resemble the entries in the McCaslin ledgers). The dates on the I.O.U.s show that Hubert had begun writing them in 1867, as he used up the gold pieces intended for his nephew. The final note—indicating simply *"One silver cup"*—was written years later, after Hubert had come with Tennie's great-grandfather to live at the McCaslin plantation because his own home, Warwick, had burned to the ground (294).

Thus, on the same day, Ike denies all McCaslin property and learns that he has inherited no Beauchamp property. There is nothing he can sacrifice as a latter-day biblical Isaac, even if he would. Sam and Carothers still speak louder to him than Cass. No longer Moses, no longer Abraham's son, he chooses to be the ultimate sacrifice of all—the Nazarene carpenter Christ (although, ironically, carpentry results in the destruction of the Big Woods that Ike professes to honor and love).

Two years later, in 1890, Ike is living in town in a rented room. He meets the daughter of his employer; her father has told her of the McCaslin plantation, she sees in the possibility of marriage to Ike her own grand inheritance. (She apparently does not know that Ike is living off of Cass and thus using the profits of the plantation he so defiantly turns against.) She easily seduces into marriage the innocent and naive Ike who, as a boy, had found Hubert's concubine both "tawdry and illicit yet somehow . . . breathless and exciting and evocative" (289), even "unforgettable" (290). But she wants a farm he cannot give her (298)—not even when, in the upper room, the would-be modern Christ is attracted to his wife's naked body and apparently attempts to impregnate her for the only time. It is her desperate gamble for high stakes—a normal and financially secure life—but to Ike, *"[S]he was born lost"* (300), as he was.

Ike adopts the form of Christ's life by living the life of a carpenter, but he does not accept its substance; as a rabbi or teacher, Jesus *suffered for* mankind. Ike, like the visionary buck, casts no shadow. Instead, he can only invoke his wife's variation on the primal scene and his primal curse when, lying on her side, she laughs (301)—not as Cass did, correctively, but as Boon did, maddened by her own loss, hopelessness, and despair. In the end, what Ike opposes, it is made clear, is life itself.

Earlier, Faulkner had written of another strained marriage, one of blacks, in "That Evening Sun." It is equally grievous, equally anguishing.[46] In that story, a black washerwoman for the Compson family, named Nancy, is mortally fearful that her estranged husband, Jesus (his actual name) is trying to kill her. She is pregnant, and Jesus suspects that a white man is responsible, because Nancy has publicly accused Mr. Stovall, a bank cashier and Baptist deacon, of failing to repay debts to her. But in a racially divided Jefferson, Jesus has little way of knowing the truth (292). Indeed, Nancy may have been raped; Jesus does not know, but he thinks so. He is equally angry with her for her life of prostitution, which she feels forced to live (or is attracted to, or finds to be all she has left; it is unclear). When Mr. Compson, not at all understanding the authentic basis of her terror, tries to comfort her by assuring her that Jesus is some distance away, perhaps with another woman, she flames out in anger: "'If he [is], I better not find out about it'" (295). Nancy would kill them both. Jesus's love and loyalty are still precious to Nancy, and so is he. But how is she to tell him, and how can he accept her?

"That Evening Sun," composed at about the same time as *The Sound and the Fury*, was first published in *American Mercury* in March 1931. But the barriers to fidelity and trust were so central a price and a feature of black-white relations that Faulkner returned to them in "The Fire and the Hearth" (chapter 2 of *Go Down, Moses*) with the relationship of the white Zack Edmonds and the mulatto Lucas Beauchamp—both descendants of L. Q. C. McCaslin—at the birth of Zack's son, Roth, in 1898. Lucas's black wife, Molly, that year nursing their first child, is awakened one night during a torrential storm to help Zack (Cass's son and successor as the head of the McCaslin plantation) and his wife deliver what would be their only child. At some danger, she goes to the big house while Lucas risks his life to fetch the doctor to care for the newborn infant and mother. Luckily, Lucas survives the mission, but he and the doctor find that Zack's wife has died in childbirth. Two days later, they are forced to bury her in the orchard of the plantation because poor weather does not permit them to get to the churchyard (46).

For the next six months, Molly remains with Zack while Lucas continues to live alone, stoking the marital fire on his and Molly's hearth in the small house that old Cass had built them before he died. Then, one day, Lucas goes to Zack to demand his wife's return. To maintain his own pride and dignity, he accuses Zack of adultery during Molly's long stay from home, despite Zack's denial and his own shame

(46–47). A grievous impasse has been reached and announced. How is Zack to prove he did not use Molly? And how can Lucas, after his visit, stop Zack—or himself, for that matter—from realizing that in his mind, he has transformed his own wife into Eunice, suspecting Zack of behavior that their shared ancestor, old Carothers, had inflicted first on Lucas's great-grandmother and then on the product of their union, Lucas's grandmother, eventually spawning him? He had thought originally to flush Zack out; he has flushed himself out as well. The hunter has become the hunted and his own worse victim. Now his only way to regain dignity is to kill Zack—to make certain he has not been made a fool and to show his own dominance with his own wife (48).

A society in which races are equal would not give rise to such fears and suspicions. But this is not a society in which races are equal, even when they are related, even after emancipation has set the black man free. Lucas's deep pain makes matters still worse when he approaches Molly and finds her nursing only one baby—the white one. He cries out in agony, again exposing himself: "'What's ourn? . . . What's mine?'" (49). He will not accept Molly's denials of any involvement with Zack or her claims that her humanity dictates that she care for the baby because Zack cannot. Instead, Lucas hopes to square things when Zack comes to take his own son back, to retrieve his dignity by forcing Zack into his earlier position of humiliation. Lucas also seeks revenge; he will let Zack know how it feels to beg.

But Zack never comes. For Lucas, this is an offense against his authority and his honor as a man. So he takes a knotted rag with coins, a real legacy he received from old Carothers (as opposed to Hubert's I.O.U.s), and places them alongside Molly, where she will find them in the morning: he too will provide a legacy for his own. Then he takes his razor and goes to meet Zack. At first light, Lucas enters Zack's unlocked house, goes to the bedroom, and stands over the sleeping man until Zack awakens. Reversing now the roles of Uncle Buck and Uncle Buddy with Tomey's Turl in "Was," Lucas gives Zack his sporting chance. He would trade Molly for his own honor, as Hubert would trade Sophonsiba for his own gain. Lucas realizes that his honor is worth more than his life; in his society, a black man who kills a white man gets lynched with no questions asked.

Once Zack is awake, he and Lucas trade racial stereotypes of fundamental mistrust. Zack asks Lucas to put away his razor; Lucas asks Zack to pull the pistol out from under his pillow. Then Lucas flings his razor away and gives Zack the opportunity to take his pistol from the dresser drawer, where he actually keeps it. Lucas is still thinking of Carothers and Eunice, of the irreversible damage his grandfather has done to his forefathers and to his family line (53). But neither Lucas nor Zack is free. Both are bound by their families, their bloodlines, their genealogy and race. Their past love and trust for each other has been annihilated; their shared idyllic childhood—shared across the races, as with Sam and Ike—is gone forever (54). Grasping Zack in what is "almost like an embrace" (56) (recalling the way in which Boon clasped Old Ben), Lucas presses the pistol into Zack's side and shoots—but the pistol misfires. It fails from disuse. The chance of insemination during intercourse made Tomasina; the chance of the gun's misfire saves her grandson.

So Lucas returns to plowing the McCaslin fields, watering and feeding the mule, and eating Molly's biscuits at noontime (57). Their child Henry will grow up with Zack's child, Roth—at least at the beginning—and in Zack's house too. The routine has been resumed. Lucas must learn to live with uncertainty, resign himself to ignorance: *"Women. I wont never know. I dont want to"* (58). Lucas has learned what Uncle Buck and Uncle Buddy, Sam, and even Cass did not learn—to let go. Like Cass, Lucas learns—as Ike never does—to live with himself and with his own severe limitations: limitations bred in the culture and bred in him. Race remains crucial, and the white race remains dominant. Next to Cass's accepted responsibilities and Lucas's struggle to find a measure of peace, Ike McCaslin's role-playing looks selfish, superficial, and foolish.

7

Now
(1921–1941)

A week earlier I had read newspaper accounts of some trouble at a place called Providence Farm, a cooperative, interracial venture in rural Mississippi that I had never heard of. There had been a meeting of white citizens at the nearby Tchula High School.

Tchula, Choctaw word for red fox, was a town of less than two thousand people, two-thirds of whom were black. The news stories reported the meeting was convened following an incident in which four Negro youths, riding on the flat-bed of a farm truck on a brisk fall morning, had frightened a third-grade white girl waiting for the school bus near Providence Farm. She had thought they whistled or hollered at her as they passed.

The alleged incident occurred only one week after Roy Bryant and J. W. Milam had been acquitted in the nearby town of Sumner by an all-male, all-white jury for the kidnapping and murder of fourteen-year-old Emmett Till. Emmett and his cousin, Curtis Jones, both from Chicago, were visiting relatives in Mississippi. They were staying with Mose Wright, Curtis's grandfather. Emmett reportedly had said, "Bye, baby," to a white woman after buying some candy in her store. He had been taken from Mose Wright's shack late at night, murdered, and thrown into the Tallahatchie River. At the trial, freed from fear by grief and anger, the grandfather of Curtis Jones stood in open court and defied what had been instilled in his people for centuries.

When asked by the prosecuting attorney if he could identify the men who had come to his door that night and demanded the youth, he stood erect in the witness stand, pointed his long, bony finger at Milam, then at Roy Bryant, and uttered two words that would go down in the annals of courage. "Thar he." Though he soon left the state forever, his doughty stand became an ongoing precept for a generation of black citizens who would be similarly challenged during the long dark night of what we remember as the civil rights movement.

"Thar he." There should be a commemorative medallion with gold lettering. There should be a national holiday. September 20. THAR HE DAY, on the calendar. An old black man, boldly accusing two murderous white men with his entire world watching, the guns of ages pointed at his heart. Yes, there should be a day. For it was a beginning.

The little girl, frightened by the talk she had heard about the Till child's murder and the rumors of Negro reprisals, was crying when the bus arrived. The driver made her tell her teacher what had happened.

The news stories had said the school principal had called the sheriff and that he had promptly arrested the four boys. John Herbers, then a correspondent for United Press, wrote that the Negro youths were questioned for two hours by Sheriff Richard Byrd, County Attorney Pat Barrett, state legislator Ed White, and local businessman William Moses. No legal counsel and no parents were present. According to the newspaper accounts, most of the questions had to do with activities at Providence Farm, where the boys sometimes visited and played. The scared youths gave incriminating responses to leading questions. Things like, "Have you ever seen colored folks in the swimming pool?" When one answered, "Yeahsuh," he was not allowed to explain that in the summer there was a day camp for Negro children and the campers went swimming. There were no white campers. The swimming pool, I learned, was nothing more than a dynamited hold below a cold, fresh-water spring. According to Mr. Cox, the only "mixed swimming" had been when a Negro nursemaid attending the Cox and Minter children went into the water with them to keep them from drowning.

The mass meeting at Tchula High School was held three nights after the youths were questioned. Newspaper accounts agreed that the White Citizens Council, an organization formed to preserve racial segregation shortly after the May 17, 1954, Supreme Court decision, was responsible for the meeting. W. F. "Bill" Minor, head of the New Orleans *Times-Picayune*'s Mississippi bureau, reported that Moses was head of the county chapter of the Citizens Council, County Attorney Barrett was president of the Lexington (county seat) chapter, and Representative J. P. Love led the Tchula chapter.

A tape recording of the interrogation was played to the approximately five hundred men and a few women present. Mr. Cox and Dr. Minter were questioned by the audience regarding their views and purpose. At the conclusion of what Editor Hodding Carter of the *Delta Democrat-Times* of Greenville described as a kangaroo court, a vote was taken, and Providence Farm was ordered to disband and the organizing families were ordered to leave the county. (Campbell, 5–7)

The years when Roth manages the McCaslin plantation, following the death of his father, Zack (1921–41), constitute the last major period of *Go Down, Moses*. Events of that period are narrated in all or parts of four chapters of the novel: "Go Down, Moses," "Delta Autumn," "Pantaloon in Black," and most of "The Fire and the Hearth." Like the rest of the novel, those chapters emphasize what C. Vann Woodward, in *The Burden of Southern History*, sees as distinctive about Southern writing generally—in Allan Tate's words, "the consciousness of the past in the present" (35). Woodward has in mind especially the testaments of 12 Southern writers who, in their 1930 manifesto *I'll Take My Stand*, saw the region distinguishing itself as the home of agrarian rather than industrial values (much as Ike argues in sections 4 and 5 of "The Bear"): "Agrarianism and its values were the essence of the Southern tradition and the test of Southern loyalty. Their credo held that 'the whole way in which we live, act, think, and feel,' the humanist culture, 'was rooted in the agrarian way of life of the older South'" (8). Part of the need for such a joint proclamation, as Woodward later points out, is that the plantation system effectively guaranteed, at least in the early years, the abolitionist movements that began in the South in the 1820s and gained considerable force until they were effectively defeated in the debates over emancipation before the Virginia legislature during its session in 1831–32: "By 1837 there was not one antislavery society remaining in the whole South" (199).

Writing from the black perspective about such matters in his history of American slavery, *Roll, Jordan, Roll*, Eugene D. Genovese sees slavery and its effects in starker terms. "Southern paternalism, like every other paternalism, had little to do with Ole Massa's ostensible benevolence, kindness, and good cheer. It grew out of the necessity to discipline and morally justify a system of exploitation. It did encourage kindness and affection, but it simultaneously encouraged cruelty and hatred. The racial distinction between master and slave heightened the tension inherent in an unjust social order" (4). The relationships between the races became even more complicated and more subtle, according to Genovese, when household servants were separated from farmhands and permitted to live or spend much of their time in the big house rather than the slave quarters (as Tomey's Turl is allowed to do). Such division of blacks increased the tension between the races and drove subtle combinations of love and resentment into subterranean practices as means of response. Thus Genovese writes that "the sources continue to hold many secrets, but the house servants appear to have been the primary agents for that cultural fusion of Africa and Europe and of diverse white and black experiences in the plantation community, which resulted, among other things, in an Afro-American Christianity and guaranteed it some influence on the religion of the whites." That influence allows the black gospel hymn, "Go Down, Moses," to suggest to Ike McCaslin one of the solutions he might himself take in confronting the tangled McCaslin-Beauchamp-Edmonds genealogy. Genovese continues,

> The house servants did not so much stand between two cultures as they remained suspended between two politics. Their intimacy with the whites more rapidly represented an exaggerated form of the master-slave relationship in general than a counterpoint to a separation of masters and field hands. As such, it drew the teeth of politically relevant class hatreds even while it nurtured no few personal hatreds. The contradictory conditions generated by so close a life with the whites provided a critical standpoint that eventually led to a desire for freedom and equality, but the very intimacy of those conditions made it difficult for most—notwithstanding the many exceptions . . . —to make a complete break. The house servants emerged as the great "integrationists" in the black community, culturally as well as politically—the one demanded the

other—but without them, the seeds of a separate nationality in the
quarters could not have sprouted in the first place. (365)

We have already seen that Ike himself found integration neither desirable nor, for some time at least, even possible; in *Go Down, Moses*,
present racial conflicts, often subtle or subterranean, nevertheless grow
out of the historical situation that Genovese has described.

Although the last chronological period of *Go Down, Moses* is
meant to cover two decades in early and mid-twentieth century, nearly
all the events Faulkner depicts are crowded into the two years during
which he was writing the novel and overseeing its publication,
1940–41—and they portray the intense power and pressure of racial
issues at the time. Whereas the first chronological period opens with a
chase after an escaped slave—Tomey's Turl, the half-brother of Uncle
Buck and Uncle Buddy as well as the grandson of their father, L. Q. C.
McCaslin—the third period opens with a Chicago manhunt for Tomey's
Turl's great-grandson, Samuel Worsham Beauchamp, whose black blood
is mixed with the white blood of the McCaslins. But "Butch"
Beauchamp is no fox, bear, or deer; he is the "slain wolf" (364) whose
rapacity ends with his execution for the murder of a Chicago policeman
in July 1940. His rebellious career, moreover, has followed the trail of
the descendants of James Beauchamp (who also abruptly departed
Jefferson) and has come to a close in the same city where his third
cousin, the granddaughter of Tennie's Jim, now lives. Despite his flight,
then, there is a curious way in which he has never been able to escape his
roots—and Molly Beauchamp (whose name is spelled "Mollie" in this
story) and Miss Belle Worsham together will see that those roots are recognized when they bring him home for burial.

When we first meet Butch in his cell, along with the census takers,
he is well dressed in the latest costly but flashy clothes, maintaining an
appearance that is at first largely heroic and even classical (351). He
seems sufficiently statuesque to rise above the petty crimes in which he
has, for most of his abbreviated life, been involved: gambling and fighting at 19, later breaking into Rouncewell's store in Jefferson and robbing
it (354). It was Roth Edmonds who discovered Butch breaking into the
McCaslin commissary to rob it and who, in angry justice, ordered him

off the plantation forever (355). Caught robbing Rouncewell's a year later, Butch is pistol-whipped by a police officer who surprises him (354), attacked with a modern weapon of aggression and abuse more successful in the policeman's hands than it had been in Lucas's when he confronted Zack a generation earlier. Butch, "not yet twenty-one," breaks out of jail two days later and flees, "with something in him," we are told by an omniscient narrator, "from the father who begot and deserted him and who was now in the State Penitentiary for manslaughter—some seed not only violent but dangerous and bad" (355). He is thus a specific example of Ike's more abstract theory of dispossession. But Butch has been dispossessed not only of family inheritance but of family too—dispossessed with no Canaan in sight. By the time of his death in Chicago, however, as Gavin Stevens reports to Miss Worsham, Butch's criminal files and Chicago newspaper accounts show that Butch had finally made money by joining the numbers racket (357). In seeking a way to restore possessions he had first sought from the McCaslin commissary, as well as position and self-respect, Butch found in the numbers conspiracy an abstract, criminal means of life that at every turn undermined and mocked Ike's smug theory of relinquishment.

Such an evident need to gather in money and to spend it ostentatiously is not only a clear example of the "double consciousness" that W. E. B. DuBois discusses, in which the subordinate race seeks approval and shows scorn by imitating the dominant culture, through whose eyes it has been trained to see success; it also, in this instance, helps us to measure the deep rage and hatred Butch feels toward the white community, even as (with violent flourish) he imitates that community. Thus, his initial classical appearance at the beginning of "Go Down, Moses" depends in part on an expensive treatment of his black hair, which contrasts with his excessive and absurd set of white men's clothes known in apparel stores and in fashion advertising as "ensembles" (351). Leon F. Litwack tells of an analogous action in his book *Been in the Storm So Long*: "Not long after the war, the wife of a former slave trader watched in horror as a freedman in Petersburg, Virginia, skinned a live catfish. Clearly upset, she asked him how he could be so cruel. 'Why, did is de way dey used to do me,' he replied, 'and I's gwine to get even wid somebody'" (199). In just a short time,

The grave of Callie Barr, a probable model for Molly Beauchamp, in the
black section of St. Peter's Cemetery in Oxford, Mississippi. The inscription,
"Her white children bless her," was written by Faulkner.
Photograph by Arthur F. Kinney.

back on the McCaslin plantation, Rider (in "Pantaloon in Black") will
know the same violent rage and disgust.

But in Jefferson now, it is Butch's own grandmother, Molly
Beauchamp, the one who raised him when his father went off to
prison, who knows this sense of violation and her grandson's authentic anger. She comes to the white lawyer Gavin Stevens for help, not
out of relinquishment or revenge but in confrontation and responsibility. She accuses Roth of selling her " 'Benjamin. . . . in Egypt. Pharaoh
got him' " and asks Gavin to help her find him (353–54). For Molly,
Butch is " '*my* Benjamin,' " " '*my* boy,' " but she believes that the
responsibility for his well-being is nevertheless the responsibility of the
white community too, and of the law that binds both communities
together. Molly may blame Roth Edmonds, but she will also enlist
those whites whose job it is to guarantee her justice and help.

Molly's principled behavior is based in love as much as in justice,
and both are made public in her insistence on a proper burial procession

in Jefferson and a proper interment for Butch. It is a situation that the white Miss Worsham understands—in part, perhaps, because she and Molly "grew up together as sisters would" (357)—a relationship that Stevens willfully ignores. Miss Worsham goes to Gavin not simply to find out more about Butch on Molly's behalf but also because she thinks of Molly as kin, and she wants to make certain that justice and concern are pursued regardless of race. On learning that Butch is dead, she insists that he receive a proper coffin: " 'Not just a box, Mr Stevens' " (358).

Miss Worsham's reproach informs and chastens Gavin as Molly's could not: this too is presented as a matter of communication between the races. But Gavin, like Ike, wishes to serve the common cause of humanity, and he in turn enlists the newspaper editor Wilmoth by command and the white business community by insistence, collecting their dollars and their loose change around the town square in order to bring Butch's body home in a coffin—which will cost far more than the precious $25 given him by Miss Worsham to " 'take care of the immediate expenses' " (359). But just as Ike betrays the roles of Moses and Christ—the roles of redemption and sacrifice and of the love of brotherhood—culture has trained Gavin to do so, too. He asks for contributions of money on behalf of the white Miss Worsham, not on behalf of " 'a dead nigger' " (360). Nor does Gavin, as the most concerned member of Jefferson's white community apart from Miss Worsham, learn any more about communal brotherhood from visiting her house on the edge of town, where he feels estranged at the very entrance (361). Indeed, the whole call of courtesy bothers and bewilders him. Molly and her brother, Hamp, recite a mournful call-and-response about the betrayal of Butch (the black man) to Pharaoh (the white man) and about his modern-day enslavement—he is " 'sold' " (362–63)—to the modern Egypt of the South and of America as well. Lost in their petitions to the Lord, they do not recognize Gavin nor welcome him in conversation. He leaves swiftly, as Miss Worsham, well mannered as always, attempts to console and instruct him: " 'It's our grief' " (363). Their understanding alone gives them the right to suffer.

Such separate, segregated racial attitudes are displayed again the following day, and again Gavin is slow to comprehend what Molly and perhaps Miss Worsham were born knowing. Butch's fabricated cortege moves "with an unctuous, an almost bishoplike purr" (364) around the town square of Jefferson while the white merchants and professional men who contributed to the cost watch silently from within their own shops and offices, their own establishments. At the edge of town, where Miss Worsham lives with Hamp and his wife and where Molly Beauchamp is now a family guest, Gavin pulls off the road with the editor. The procession passes a sign that reads "Jefferson. Corporate Limit" (364), thus entering another territory that, having been established by the white community, now provides limits on their corporate state. Like Ike, Gavin had thought that giving (or giving up) money would remove such restrictions—at least temporarily—and give him a new dignity and freedom. Clearly, it did not.

Yet if Butch Beauchamp embodies the rage that governed much of the life and philosophy of Malcolm X in the years that followed 1940 and that now plays its stern role in the person of Louis Farrakhan and his separatist Nation of Islam, Molly embodies a counterstatement that is reminiscent of Martin Luther King, Jr., who argued the necessity of seeing all peoples locked into a single garment of destiny.[47] "'I wants hit all in de paper. All of hit'" Molly commands Wilmoth (365); surprised, he also vaguely comprehends—Butch's guilt is not his alone but a communal guilt, and the whites shall know too what it means to lack a redeemer in this world. They must not escape their own role, beginning with Butch's dismissal at the hands of Roth and going back beyond that, back beyond Ike to old Carothers as a cultural embodiment of the force that has bred them all. Wilmoth's struggle to understand and his quick acquiescence to Molly's desire is just the sort of response that Molly—and Miss Worsham—want. In a world without Moses, it is a small sign of hope.

Next to Wilmoth's response, Gavin's reaction (365) is not only disappointing; it is devastating. As a self-styled humanitarian and liberal, Gavin—whose perception is that Molly is concerned only with appearances and form—is as blind as the white men in Chicago who see only superficially the significance of Butch's fawn-colored clothes. This incident in Jefferson in July 1940 does not merely condemn the attitudes of well-intentioned whites like Gavin. What it really asks—

acutely, forcefully—is, if Moses (or his disciple) were to come to Jefferson, would Gavin Stevens (and his kind) ever recognize him?

Three months later, in November 1940, this question is still central in chapter 6 of *Go Down, Moses*, "Delta Autumn," wherein Ike's vision of "the best game of all, the best of all breathing and forever the best of all listening" (184) is sharply compromised by talk of the advance of Adolf Hitler and World War II and by references to Roth Edmond's "doe" (321). But the annual hunting trip has for Ike long been a much-diminished thing. Now, to find any woods fit for hunting, he and "two of the sons of his old companions" (320)—Will Legate and Roth—must drive 200 miles. Along the way, they must pass plantations such as the one Ike repudiated—constant reminders for him of the ongoing possession of land and of blacks to farm it, this time for markets throughout the world—and he is resentful (324). The woods that had given Ike a sense of special privilege as a boy have now become opaque, and he senses a growing alienation (326).

His thoughts are abruptly interrupted when, seeing something on the road, Roth Edmonds, his third cousin and the current head of the McCaslin plantation, brings the car to a sudden stop (320–21). When Ike asks what's the matter, Roth snaps, "'I didn't intend to come back here this time'" (321). Ike is puzzled, but Legate is not: he remarks that Roth's "'got a doe'" in the woods, "'one that walks on two legs'" (321). Then Ike remembers Roth's suspicious overnight disappearance the year before.

To divert the conversation, Ike brings up Hitler—who seems to hunt men, not animals, unconscionably—and suggests that such a menace might also appear in America under some other name. Whatever any such man might call himself, Legate says, Americans will stop him. When Roth indicates that he is not at all certain that Legate is right, Ike is suddenly dismissive in a spasm of nationalism (322–23). In struggling to cling, through a revised interpretation of his old notion, to his fundamental belief in "'the communal anonymity of brotherhood'" (246), Ike makes Uncle Buck equivalent to Hitler, whom he groups with George Washington, Franklin D. Roosevelt, and Wendell Willkie.

General Stone's hunting camp, a model for "Delta Autumn."
Photograph by Arthur F. Kinney.

Although we know that Faulkner was deeply troubled by the
looming danger of a world war during one of his own hunting trips at
the time, such a connection would never have entered his fiction unless
he had a deeper point to make. What Ike's sudden reference to Hitler
suggests—since nothing in the conversation has prompted it—is his
own deep psychological struggle and obsession with genealogy.

Like Ike (and perhaps like Faulkner), Hitler too was profoundly
worried about his ancestry. Hitler's father was illegitimate, and his
grandmother never told him (she may never have known for certain)
who his actual grandfather was. Because his grandmother was a
domestic servant to a Jewish family, the Frankenbergers, and since
Herr Frankenberger gave her monthly child support for 14 years for
young Adolf, Hitler was obsessed not only with his own illegitimacy
but also with the likelihood that the father whose identity was hidden
from him was actually Jewish and refused to admit his paternity except
by this means of a private cash arrangement. Like Ike, then, who

strives to repress the miscegenation in his own family past and the illegitimate Beauchamp line that has descended from it, Hitler worried about his own family history, which was also characterized by illegitimacy and mixed bloodlines. And like Ike, Hitler spun his own philosophy of family and racial purity in his insistence on Aryanism, in order to erase and repudiate his own personal past. For Hitler, as for Ike, the mixture of bloodlines was the original sin, a legacy that demanded of him a life of penance and organized change. Legate's cheap shots about Roth's "'light-colored'" does, then (321), and Roth's promise to stop hunting them (322), trigger in Ike thoughts and fears that have clearly haunted him since the day he left the McCaslin plantation.

But Roth is haunted, too, as revealed by his remarks on America as a country plagued by mismanagement, a country of haves and have-nots, teeming with discontent (323). Legate's insistence on crudely taunting Roth about doe hunting is just as insistently converted by Ike, then, into something more acceptable to this titular head of the family—a comment on the value of fighting on behalf of women and children (323). Roth's cynical reply—"'Haven't you discovered . . . that women and children are one thing there's never any scarcity of?'"—surely grows out of his own despair and sense of self-hatred as much as from his discouragement over having been burdened with the responsibility of managing the family plantation with no help from Ike or anyone else. But it is a sentiment that Ike cannot afford to recognize, because to do so would be to admit the failed wisdom of his own decision to leave the land to Cass Edmonds and his descendants. Through shared knowledge of a potent analogy far more sophisticated and penetrating than Legate's, Roth and Ike speak at desperate cross-purposes, much as Cass and Ike once did in the commissary. Most dangerously, Ike has changed the terms of his argument in this encoded debate, from conscience and guilt (for all men, he says, can—and will?—be better) to honor and shame. This marks a sad and somewhat disappointing surrender by Ike to an old aristocratic culture he had once meant dramatically to disown.

That night, in camp, Ike lies sleepless in his cot (327, 333), reiterating his past decision and the events that followed it (334–35) and finding peace in the creation of yet another self-centered myth, in which he sees himself and the woods at one—their existence suitable, poetically coterminous, "two spans running out together, . . . where the wild strong immortal game ran forever before the tireless belling immortal hounds" (337–38).

In the morning, Roth again jolts Ike into present reality when he suddenly appears with a mission for his older relative, the head of his clan. Roth expects a " 'messenger' " to appear at camp, and he wants Ike to give the visitor an envelope and a message: " '[T]ell h—. . . . Tell her No' " (339). Whether this decision by Roth is an act of repudiation or one of evasion and cowardice—and therefore parallels Ike's own repudiation to Roth's grandfather in the McCaslin commissary more than a half-century earlier—Roth is really offering Ike a second chance to accept responsibility for the McCaslin past. In December 1885 Ike had tried to pay a legacy to James Beauchamp and failed; now, in November 1940, he is given money to pay Tennie's Jim's granddaughter, although her identity has not yet been revealed.

But Ike's myopia continues; he sees neither his opportunity nor the dark irony. When the woman enters his tent unannounced, he is quick to see that she is carrying a baby and that it is Roth's (340). But her reaction to the envelope is the same as Fonsiba's husband's reaction in 1886: " 'That's just money,' she said" (341). Like her grandfather and his sister before her, she will not be bought off. She is neither grudging nor spiteful; instead, her own sense of dignity recalls her past joy with Roth and their mutual agreement. She had promised Roth no entangling alliances, and he had not promised her marriage, although he did (as old Carothers did, in his way) provide support for her and now the child. But this redefinition of honor as mutual respect— shared, natural, and nearly spontaneous, agreed to by both parties—is something Ike cannot understand. For him, there must be a bargain struck, gains received, belying his own dependence on the monthly allowance he had received for more than a half-century—first from Cass, then from Zack, now from Roth—against the inheritance he had claimed to relinquish. " 'What do you want?' " he demands of the woman. " 'What do you expect?' " (342).

In reply, she recounts the ancestral history that brings all of them within a single narrative and genealogical orbit (342–43). But she finds little reaction in Ike, so she gives the tale the sting of a stronger truth:

"'I would have made a man of him. He's not a man yet. You spoiled him. You, and Uncle Lucas and Aunt Mollie. But mostly you'" (343). Ike is swift to deny any responsibility or obligation here, too. Instead, he parries her thrust, blaming her family, not the McCaslins or the Edmondses. When, in the course of her account of her own lineage, she mentions that the aunt with whom she had been living took in washing, he cries out the realization that strikes his rigid and still-prejudicial mind: "'You're a nigger!'" (343–44).

"'Yes,' she [replies]. 'James Beauchamp—you called him Tennie's Jim though he had [his own] name—was my grandfather. I said you were Uncle Isaac'" (344). Thus she identifies herself not by Roth but by Isaac, not by the Edmondses but by the Beauchamps and, behind and within them, the McCaslins. But like Gavin, who gives no name to the dead "nigger" in "Go Down, Moses" until Miss Worsham tells him he has a name (358), the young woman who has borne Roth's child must remind Ike that James Beauchamp, too, had a patronymic line. And having turned the plantation over to Roth, she tells Ike, he must bear some of the blame for any of Roth's subsequent behavior (343). Such behavior is yet another act of miscegenation, and in the paternity largely denied by Roth in his refusal to marry the woman, Ike sees that old Carothers's behavior had been enacted again: the wheel has come full circle, and the McCaslin name (like Du Homme) is its own doom.

The situation made clear to him at last, Ike dismisses the woman as suddenly and sternly as Cass had dismissed Fonsiba's husband-to-be (344, 264). Yet he calls her back to pay her off—first with Roth's money (344–45) and then, with some physical effort, the precious hunting horn that General Compson had willed him (346). The latter gesture, as useless to the baby as it is thought generous by Ike, is at any event *cheaper than saying My* [niece] *to a nigger"* (258).

The woman, in her obvious love and respect for Roth, can appreciate not only his corruption at the hands of Ike but also his corruption at the hands of his culture. He was brought up in a household where, we shall learn, he felt restricted and, in time, unable to mingle freely even with Henry, his black foster brother, who was Roth's best friend in his early years (107). The woman's depth of compassion is matched with a visionary range far beyond Ike's failing capacities.

Now

To avoid blaming her or her race, Ike might well have turned to his equally facile theory of gender—"[W]omen hope for so much," he had earlier told himself (335)—had it not been made irrelevant by the woman who stands before him. So like old Carothers marrying off the pregnant Eunice, he gives her his own best avuncular advice: return to the North, forget Roth, and complete her family by marrying a black man to raise the child. It is a speech stunning in its regressiveness—making Ike Carothers all over again—and in its audacity and its total misunderstanding. By only the most stubbornly blind and deaf of responses could he associate this woman with "'revenge'" (346); Ike's advice, reflecting his thought, is still based in the worst kind of patronizing, racial stereotypes. It stoutly denies all that the woman has said, recalled, and implied. Now it is her turn to blaze forth at this final instance of a McCaslin invoking McCaslin privilege, something far cruder than the culturally, economically, and historically restricted Roth has ever proposed to her. She tells Ike what she could find no reason to tell Roth: that even in old age, he is a man who has never known nor understood love (346). Then she is forever gone.

Alone now in his cot, "trembling, panting" (347), shivering in the morning cold, Ike retreats from all involvement in the world—returning in his mind to Sam's mythical sense of holy origins, spun into a wider historical theory based on the exploitation of later settlers, to free himself totally and forever (347). In his apocalyptic view, the woods are destroyed forever; whites go to Memphis whorehouses nightly; blacks own plantations and mansions in Chicago; Aryans breed with Jews. It is a nightmarish vision that might serve as Ike's epitaph—a devastating self-exposure revealing the bankruptcy of his cultural obligation and values. And yet, if we were forced to choose between being Gavin Stevens or Ike McCaslin in 1940—although that is hardly a choice anyone would willingly make—we might choose Ike. He at least recognizes that something, somewhere has gone dreadfully wrong. He no longer has Gavin's smug white contentment.

Nearly a year later, in August 1941, the relative ineptitude of whites—the complacency of Gavin, the troubled guilt of Roth, the hopelessness of Ike—gives way to active black rage when, in chapter 3,

"Pantaloon in Black," Rider's wife, Mannie, suddenly and inexplicably dies. In its barest outlines, "Pantaloon in Black" is, like "Dry September" and *Light in August*, another narrative of lynching, showing that the wounds of the historic deaths of Nelse Patton and Elwood Higginbotham (see Appendix II) had still not healed—at least not for Faulkner. But it is a much deeper and more daring story than that, for unlike anything before or after, it is Faulkner's sole attempt to get into the mind of a repressed black consciousness. That he does so with limited conceptual and verbal agility does not diminish the power of his episode nor its crucial placement in *Go Down, Moses*. Rider, too, seeks Moses without success.

We first see Rider's strong and impressive frame at the age of 24 when, grief-stricken, he insists on singlehandedly finishing his wife's burial once her coffin is lowered into the ground (131). He refuses alike the companionship and solace of his family (like Roth and Ike, he is raised by surrogate parents, his aunt and uncle) and members of his crew at the sawmill (133). Instead, he returns to the cabin he rents from Roth Edmonds, where he had made Mannie a fire on the hearth on their wedding night (in imitation of Lucas and Molly Beauchamp, Roth's oldest tenants) and where he and Mannie had toiled, in their six months of marriage, to give themselves a better life. Mannie is, for the first time and forever, absent, but the depth of his love and the power of his anguish temporarily will her ghost back to solace him: it is an extraordinary act of union with a spouse, not a buck, that would puzzle and shame Ike McCaslin.

The next morning, returning to work, Rider still finds solace beyond reach. Even the supreme effort of raising and tossing, without the aid of a cant hook, a log more gigantic than any he had ever moved alone (141–42) fails to distract him from the aching of his heart and mind. This newly reformed and responsible black worker and husband, victimized by chance death, can find no outlet. Like Rider, we are not permitted to know the cause of Mannie's death—nor is anyone else. Instead, we, like Rider, are put into his victimized position, baffled by events and searching for a response—in a black culture where the possibilities are limited.

His marriage having dissolved, Rider turns to the rituals that had sustained him before he met Mannie. He goes at night to buy moonshine

A lumber mill in Enterprise, Mississippi, a possible model for Faulkner's
"Pantaloon in Black."
Photograph by Arthur F. Kinney.

from an unshaven white man (142). Their confrontation is pronouncedly racial, and it is clear that Rider has been dependent on this white
bootlegger for some time. When he finally gets the liquor and walks
away, gulping it from his jug, he sees his aunt's husband approaching. As
he had earlier, the old man implores Rider to " 'come home' " (144).
Finally, Rider complies, returning to the house in which he was raised.
There, his aunt attempts to offer religious consolation, but Rider denies
that too (146); it is a comfort of whites, from what is fundamentally a
white religion, and it has now failed him. Moving swiftly on, continuing
to drink, he comes once more to the sawmill. He walks through the boil-
er-shed and into the tool-room, where he intrudes on a game of craps,
demanding to play. The one white man there, running the game, is the
sawmill's night watchman. " 'You're drunk,' " he says to Rider. " 'One of
you niggers . . . get him out of here' " (147). But Rider joins the game
anyway—a game that is clearly crooked.

In his high and raw emotional state, Rider connects the white
man's absolute control of moonshine with the failure of the white

man's religion to comfort him, despite his uncle's and aunt's promises. He then connects both with the white man whose dominance in throwing the dice and in organizing the game seems especially contrived. Rider grasps the man by the wrist—and a second pair of dice fall to the floor (148). As the white man springs to his feet, backs away, and reaches for his pistol, Rider leaps forward in a movement of strength, precision, and grace. "In the second before the half-drawn pistol explode[s]," Rider forcefully punches the white man's throat and then, with his razor, makes a single, clean incision in it (148–49), recalling Sam Fathers's slitting of the deer's throat before young Isaac. But this is not sport—not even serious and instructive sport. The act is neither random nor selfish. In killing the white man who has been cheating him for years, Rider also rids the mill of the white night watchman who has continually preyed on Rider's black world.

There has been considerable preparation for this act; it is the accumulated effect of all the wounds and scars, indignities and suffering that the black Rider has suffered repeatedly at the hands of the dominant white race. At the same time, he finds a way to vent his rage that is revelatory, if not wholly constructive, for his fellow workers: he makes himself a sacrificial victim by his own choosing, not by God's or the white man's. The anger and pessimism that slavery, Jim Crow segregation, and exploitation have bred in Rider come rushing forth. If his act is also a suicidal urge, a desperate attempt to rejoin Mannie, it is only partly that: what Rider strikes out against is a world characterized by unfairness—the unfairness of Mannie's death, the unfairness of a racist culture, and, we will soon learn, the unfairness of a legal system that does not provide equal protection under the law.

But Rider shares the role of protagonist with the white deputy sheriff who is asked to apprehend him and protect him against the night watchman's family, the Birdsongs, while sufficiently keeping the peace so as not to disrupt the chances of the sheriff, Maydew, of being reelected. The unnamed deputy is able to arrest Rider the next day, because by chance he finds him asleep at his house. Rider does not resist arrest; he does, however, resist imprisonment. Once locked in jail—feeling trapped, placed in bondage—he rips the cot from the floor and the cell door from the wall and walks out. He is brought under control again, this time by a black chain gang who share his cell and who take him to the ground under the direction of Ketcham, the prison guard, who refuses to shoot him because he wishes the Birdsongs to have their chance. Rider is found the next day, swinging "from the bellrope in a negro schoolhouse about two miles from the sawmill," which places the death on or near the McCaslin plantation; the coroner's verdict is "death at the hands of a person or persons unknown" (149).

The events after Rider's arrest are narrated in retrospect by the deputy of the sheriff to his wife. Earlier that day, she had excused herself from a card game in which she had been found cheating, as Birdsong himself had cheated; she is now consumed with preparing supper in time to see a picture show and pays no attention to her husband's account. But what matters is not what the deputy sheriff says but the obsessive way in which he keeps wrestling with the *meaning* of his story—which on the surface follows most details of a ritual lynching. Rider's behavior has troubled him deeply (149–50). Baffled, he is crude and clumsy in trying to understand a fellow human being by means of his own inadequate concept of blacks and an inadequate vocabulary to describe what he feels, yet a sure inner sense of the depth of Rider's own passion and pain. The deputy is Faulkner's strongest and finest portrait of the poor white who struggles to understand a world that cultural stereotypes and racial prejudice have forever closed to him—an early sketch of what will become the entire Gowrie family in his later novel of Lucas Beauchamp, *Intruder in the Dust.* At the same time that Faulkner insists we understand what it is like to be a black in a white society, he is also insisting that we get inside a white man whose every instinct is right but whose breeding has closed the door to sufficient understanding.

Like Rider, the deputy has just experienced something very important, if incomprehensible—and like Rider, he strives to understand. Nothing Rider does fits the conduct the deputy has been trained to expect of blacks. Everywhere Rider challenges his compassion and throws up to him his own ignorance. He recalls Rider shoveling dirt into his wife's grave as soon as the box was lowered, returning to work early the next day and performing feats of great strength, walking off the job in midafternoon and getting drunk, returning to the mill that night and killing a white man (150–51), and then going home to await apprehension. It is not that Rider's actions were sense*less*; it is just that together, they don't *make* sense. The deputy even dismisses his earlier reductive theory that blacks are inhuman; it is clear, in the way he keeps going over the events, that at some deep level he recognizes how very human Rider's actions were. He concludes his anxious examination with a sudden breakthrough of knowledge, completely lost on his wife, as he quotes Rider's final words (as reported by Ketcham): " 'Hit look lack Ah just cant quit thinking. Look lack Ah just cant quit' " (154). Rider's legacy, at his death, is to pass on that condition to the deputy, who has taken it up compulsively, seemingly against his will.

What Rider had responded to was the thought of *his* condition— defined by his widowerhood, his racial limitations, and the apparently mindless enmity of the world around him. He is trapped by his culture, as enslaved as his progenitors, doomed to bondage. What Rider has taught the deputy is his own lack of empowerment before his wife, the legal and political system, the customs of his society, and his own limited understanding. The deputy lacks the experience that Miss Worsham and Roth have had, yet he, like them, is working his way to a new understanding of his own condition and the condition of those, especially the blacks, around him. His unspoken, as yet dimly perceived point, of course, is that in fact blacks *are* human. In this story about a black man, it is his legacy to a redneck white man that is its point and its hope.

Gavin Stevens accepts the project of bringing "a dead nigger" home; Ike McCaslin sends a black woman and her baby son, who will carry on the tainted Beauchamp-Edmonds line, back North. The enraged Butch Beauchamp makes his own cage just as much as Rider does. But the intensity of these events is magnified by our awareness that they occur so close to our own present time. Weaving in, through, and around "Pantaloon in Black" are the remaining episodes of chapter 2, "The Fire and the Hearth," which begin in the spring of 1941 and conclude in October. They set Roth off against the deputy and Rider, yet Roth is an unspoken presence in all of these episodes: he has been sending money to his third cousin in Chicago and learning of her pregnancy when Butch Beauchamp, the young black he exiled from the McCaslin plantation, is brought back for a public burial in "Go Down, Moses"; in "The Fire and the Hearth," Roth must contend with Lucas and watch Lucas's effect on Molly as the Birdsongs lynch one of his tenants on or near his own land. Through this trying period, as for long years before it, however, he would pass Molly Beauchamp's house while overseeing his crops and, "see[ing] her sitting on the gallery, her shrunken face collapsed," deliver her tobacco and candy each month (96). The apparently casual, even harmless ritual actually belies Roth's very deep feelings and needs. For Molly is "the only mother he ever knew" (97); she brought him into the world, suckled him, and raised him until he was 12. Now she is even more than his mother; she is now his entire family.

When Roth was seven, "the old curse of his fathers . . . descended to him" one night, although "[h]e did not recognize it then" (107). He "beat" Molly's son, Henry Beauchamp, by taking the bed in the room where the two boys customarily slept and leaving Henry alone on the pallet they usually shared—bedding meant for blacks and slaves (108). Soon after, Molly taught Roth the bitter shame of that curse. After a month of estrangement from Henry, his childhood friend and foster brother, Roth, "in grief . . . and shame" (109), tried rapprochement. He went to the Beauchamp cabin and announced that he had come to eat supper with Molly and her family, only to have Molly serve him separate food at a separate table, alone (109–10). In doing so, Molly taught Roth what it meant to be white.

But that is not the only bitter fruit of the McCaslin heritage with which Roth knowledgeably grew up. In his teens, he learned that Lucas had confronted his father, Zack Edmonds, over his suspected treatment of Molly after Roth's own mother died in childbirth, and had won Molly back.

Edmonds, he thought, harshly and viciously. *Edmonds. Even a nigger McCaslin is a better man, better than all of us. Old Carothers got his nigger bastards right in his back yard and I would like to have seen the husband or anybody else that said him nay.*—

*Yes, Lucas beat him, else Lucas wouldn't be here. If father had
beat Lucas, he couldn't have let Lucas stay here even to forgive
him. It will only be Lucas who could have stayed because Lucas is
impervious to anybody, even to forgiving them, even to having to
harm them.* (112)

From his childhood, then, Roth recognizes that he has been compromised—by Carothers, by his father, by his mother's death, by his foster
parents—even by Ike, who transfers to Roth the responsibility of the
plantation and the cost of his monthly allowance to be free of it. Roth's
life has thus been, from the start, as difficult and complex as that of any
of the McCaslins, Beauchamps, or Edmonds. In countless subtle ways,
his heritage and his legacy have forever constrained him, hedged in his
freedom with their own customs of bondage.

This explains the final central portrait that the chronologically
presented novel yields up to us. It is the portrait of a white man who
feels forced to dismiss his own foster mother's grandson, whom Molly
has been rearing as a latter-day Roth or Henry—a white man who
learns (at what point in time?) that the woman he loves is descended
from the black McCaslin line, spawned from the first cousin of the
man whom he is supporting as a carpenter in Jefferson. This, too, is
the white man who must confront an apparently senile Lucas
Beauchamp, who has betrayed his directions and his trust for the past
twenty years and audaciously challenged his authority by placing a hidden still on his very property and making money off his secret and ille-
gal enterprise.

Like Cass Edmonds, his grandfather, Roth has elected to
immerse himself in the toil of this world and of the McCaslin plantation, facing all of the family obligations that have come down to him
alone from his widower father. Amid such deeper concerns, both long-
standing and new, Roth must find Lucas's contest with George Wilkins
in the spring of 1941 foolish and irritating, just as Lucas in his turn is
annoyed with George Wilkins, whose constant indiscretion and inferi-
or moonshine threaten his own safety (34–35). Lucas's persistent sense
of superiority over George—he does not realize that George is tricking
him into approving George's marriage to Lucas's granddaughter Nat

and providing a good dowry for her—is matched by his sense of superiority to Roth (36). Lucas chafes at having to play Sambo to Roth, seemingly unaware of Roth's own tolerant yet deeply conflicted attitude toward him.

Lucas, who means at any cost to preserve his independence, decides to hide his own still and to expose that of George Wilkins as a decoy (61). But in his attempt to secrete his own still under an Indian burial mound, he discovers quite by accident a single gold coin (38). It is unusually precious to Lucas—not simply because it is gold but also because he thinks it is part of his monetary legacy from old Carothers McCaslin, the man who had enslaved and impregnated his grandmother and great-grandmother on this very land: "the rest of it might be scattered anywhere beneath the cave-in" (39). What the elderly Lucas seems to have forgotten is that at his own request, on the day he turned 21, all the legacy money was turned over to him by Ike McCaslin, who took him to the bank to transfer it into an account in Lucas's name (105–6). Now, in his addled mind, Lucas imagines that "old Buck and Buddy had buried [the money] almost a hundred years ago" (39–40). Recalling that a few years ago some white men and women were seen digging in the same site (37), he is convinced that there is much more treasure to be found.

It is not that Lucas simply feels fated or thinks he is destined for wealth, nor even that he is bitten by greed and capitalist rapacity, like the whites in Jefferson or like Butch Beauchamp. Rather, he believes that the discovery of treasure will set him free at last from his long personal history of bondage to the McCaslin plantation, although it will cost him the love of land and pride in farming that mean so very much to him (42)—real sacrifices, unlike Ike's. Tellingly, decisively, his emancipation will come at last, and not merely at the hands of federal white law, but with Confederate wealth. At the age of 67, he will be free at last of the degenerating distaff line of McCaslins (42–43).

Ironically, to free himself, he must eventually ask the help, if not the partnership, of George Wilkins, the "fool innocent of discretion" (35) whose bootlegging has led Lucas to hide his own still. But Lucas does not understand all this at first; at first, he wishes to expose George, and to do so he must play Sambo to Roth and to the sheriff

(58). It is just this sort of posturing, this insincerity, that the conflicted Roth cannot abide. But Lucas's act backfires; George, the tricked, out-tricks the trickster. With the help of Nat, Lucas's youngest child, who saw her father burying his still (40–41), George digs Lucas's still out of the Indian mound and places it on Lucas's porch, where in due course it is discovered by the law. In the end, both Lucas and George are arrested.

So transported is Lucas by the thought of wealth leading to free-dom—betraying a deeper, if unexpressed, desire than he has shown elsewhere—that he forgets, in his game with George, things that an Uncle Buddy would never forget at poker, although Rider apparently did at craps: (1) George can always expose Lucas first (61), and (2) George can always contain Lucas by marrying Nat, something that Roth has to warn Lucas (59). To protect himself from George's testi-mony against him and to ensure Nat's cooperation, Lucas permits the marriage. But again the hunter is the hunted; the confidence man is conned. Nat will agree to the marriage, she says, only if Lucas will pro-vide as her dowry a new back porch, a cook-stove, and a well as improvements to George Wilkins's property (67–68). The repairs, she suggests, will be made by George himself. But George will no more allow his wife to run his life than Lucas will allow Molly to run his. George gets the last word—at least temporarily—by taking Lucas's dowry for Nat and buying with it a new still with which to resume his own whiskey-making operation (75). His stubbornness may only be samboism as a sham; he may actually be the cleverest operator of the three of them, despite his shuffling and indolent attitude.

Roth puts up the bail money to free George and Lucas, and by August they have undertaken a collaborative venture to find the trea-sure buried in the Indian mound. Neither one of them seems to be concerned with the sacredness of such mounds, although Faulkner surely was aware of it through articles written by friends and through reference works he doubtless consulted (Grimwood, 262–63). The blasphemy of invading religious ground is doubled, or tripled, when Lucas decides to make use of a divining machine (79). Although Roth refuses to advance him the $300 he needs to buy the machine, Lucas's excitement at the prospect of unearthing a fortune inspires him to try conning the salesman he has summoned to the plantation. He first offers the salesman half of whatever the two of them find at the site, and then offers to swap "his" mule (actually Roth's) for the machine in order to use it that night, with the promise that he will buy the mule back for $300 (80). But in his very livelihood of peddling a divining machine, the salesman himself is a con artist, and he is quick to test Lucas's right to the mule. In turn, Lucas has tricks left of his own: a map to the treasure, which he pretends to have had all along and to have misread (88–89), and a salting trick by which he plants his own money to persuade the salesman that there really is more treasure to be found and that they now have the correct location (90–94). Through this last trick, Lucas is able to turn the tables on the salesman by renting the divining machine back to him. Such devious gamesmanship, however, of the sort that led to wagers between Uncle Buck and Uncle Buddy against Hubert, or, closer, the more deadly wager between Lucas and Zack at an earlier time, is halted by Roth (95) because it distracts Lucas from his responsibilities as a tenant farmer sharecropping on the McCaslin plantation—and, surely, because it takes him from his responsibility to Molly, too, keeping him away from her even at night.

Molly is disturbed, even frightened, by Lucas's madness—and by his blasphemous digging in sacred earth at the expense of everything else, with no respect for the land, for burial rights, or for his own sacred obligation to farm his land. Moreover, she fears that he may actually find money that is not his to take (99). She tells Roth she wants to leave Lucas. Roth cannot persuade Molly to bide her time, and as her fear mounts, so does Roth's own anguish, for he sees her marriage dissolving before him. At the same time, Roth cannot questions or deny Lucas's independence, and he cannot disallow Lucas's right to farm his legacy of McCaslin land or to search for the fortune that he imagines will set him free of McCaslins and Edmondses forever—nor can Molly.

Roth makes a final attempt to convince Lucas that "'there aint any money buried around here'" (116) and to persuade him that he is too old to be working so hard at finding it. Surprisingly, Lucas finally seems to listen to reason: he says he will give the divining machine to George Wilkins. But Molly is not comforted by that promise—she cries out to Roth that Lucas would only continue to use the machine "'just the same as if had kept it'" (118). Certain that Lucas is irreversibly obsessed with his search for the money, she insists that she wants him to keep the machine—and pleads with Roth to let her divorce Lucas.

Roth responds by refusing her request and ordering Lucas to hand the machine over to him by the next morning (118). Lucas, however, does not comply. So Molly follows Roth's earlier, hypothetical suggestion (100) and takes up the divining machine herself (despite its mocking name), to show Lucas by example rather than by precept how dangerous and sinful his search is. She barely survives the ordeal, collapsing in the heat of the day, the machine that would invade nature clutched in her hand. After she recovers, Roth painfully and reluctantly agrees to grant the divorce.

It is Lucas who finally makes things right again; at the divorce proceedings, he arrives to ask Molly to reconsider, and she agrees to withdraw her application, supported—with great relief, we may imagine—by Roth (124–25). Now Lucas, not Roth, gives candy to the toothless Molly for her to gum (125). And Lucas takes the final step, too: he turns the machine over to Roth and asks him to destroy it (126–27). Occurring at the chapter's close, in October 1941, this is the last event in the novel's chronology; Lucas follows Isaac in learning the lesson of relinquishment and repudiation.

Given this humorous twist at the end, we may find that "The Fire and the Hearth," as a tale of endless, if hapless, shenanigans, fits neatly a novel that begins with another tall tale, "Was." But as noted earlier, "Was" is, past its surface level, a very serious examination of the conditions and effects of slavery, even when humorously portrayed. Likewise, on its surface, "The Fire and the Hearth" is about Lucas's decades of quiet anger and of yearning to breathe free; but it is also, more deeply, about the curse of the McCaslins and of their land, a legacy that has divided them from one another and robbed them all—the McCaslins, the Beauchamps, and the Edmondses—of any possibility of brotherhood.

The inherited family curse is the racial division that old Carothers's selfish, dominant racial privilege had initiated. Now, in the

A Mississippi farmer working the mule, as in "The Fire and the Hearth."
Photograph by Arthur F. Kinney.

struggling good will of Roth, the surrender of Lucas, and the tolerance of Molly, there are great small acts of reunion. Cornel West has recently written that "the major enemy of black survival in America has been and is neither oppression nor exploitation but rather the nihilistic threat—that is, loss of hope and absence of meaning" (15). The reconciliation of Beauchamps and Edmondses makes Molly and Roth—apparently estranged a year previously, at the time of the death of Samuel Worsham Beauchamp—pivotal in *Go Down, Moses* in combatting the "absence of meaning." There is also a renewal of hope: alongside the "solitary" Roth (125), Nat Beauchamp Wilkins is pregnant, and her first child is expected in the spring of 1942—just beyond the end of the novel. Here, then, in the turmoil of the present, where Ike's and Roth's lines seem to have come to an end, the first of a new line, the Wilkins line, is about to be born. The Beauchamps, bred from the McCaslins, continue to breed and to make that possible, too—by refusing, from Cass onward, to give up on their responsibilities to the land of their forefathers and their obligations to the white and black members of their miscegenated family. Even the last and arguably the least of them, Roth, has performed his duties as a descendant of his namesake, old Carothers, well. But as a true foster son of the Beauchamps, he has done so despite—and perhaps also because of—the curse of the South and the peculiar institution that so affected it. Perhaps there is yet reason to hope for Moses.

8

Conclusion

Go Down, Moses is only ostensibly the saga of the McCaslin family. Outwardly, it may still be about Lucius Quintus Carothers McCaslin's arrogance and greed, which led to dominance and to miscegenation; about his sons' half-hearted attempts and, in the last analysis, failure at reparation for what they increasingly perceive as wrong, if not evil; and about his grandson's extreme revulsion and similar ineptitude in total relinquishment of family responsibility once an attempt is made to pay off his black kin with their respective legacies, now tripled by his father and uncle. Within this saga there is a deeper and darker investigation of the causes and effects of racism—effects that are historical, sociological, psychological, and economic in their fundamental inhumanity and, in Faulkner's hands, the chief resource for powerful and memorable work, in part because of the forces and paradoxes that inspire and inform it. "*Go Down, Moses* voices the concern of conscience over the Negro's plight in a white man's world, yet it voices too the grief of conscience over its own helplessness," Melvin Backman writes. "The South that denies the Negro his manhood denies the white man his right to love" (174).

As we have seen, racial division and racial mixing from acts of miscegenation abort any hope for full humanity for either race in a racially oriented and racially fraught society such as Faulkner's Yoknapatawpha and preclude what Ike most desires: the communal anonymity of brotherhood—a union so strong and a concord so complete and invulnerable that all men and women are made selfless by serving the common good of everyone. *Go Down, Moses* is a novel that at once urges such a hope and, at the same time, exposes human fallibility and helplessness. Ike may propose such shibboleths, and so may Gavin Stevens, but Faulkner is too honest to let them remain before us for long, quick to deny their possibility and even their efficacy. It is a central part of Faulkner's unflinching insight—and here his achievement through fiction—to show how every character in *Go Down, Moses* is to some degree victimized by his or her cultural heritage, by custom and tradition that have taken impervious root and fossilized over time. This is true of both whites and blacks, no matter how often they chase down their ancestry and genealogy in an attempt to understand and isolate causes for such bondage (or attempt, through willed ignorance, to endure despite it).

Faulkner's novel is not, however, one of total despair, precisely because of the range of his characters' responses. If some of them—Carothers McCaslin, for example; Uncle Buck, Uncle Buddy, and Ike; Gavin Stevens; the Birdsong family—contribute to and even exacerbate racism despite their ideas and intentions, others—Fonsiba's husband, Molly Beauchamp, Miss Worsham, Cass Edmonds, Roth, Rider, an unnamed white sheriff's deputy—struggle to free their whole society from its continued enslavement to predispositions of caste, class, and race. Their degree of success, like their motives, is mixed, but all of them are meant to be instructive: characters whose fictional ideas and actions have historical import.

This much is now clear. But deconstructing the novel that Faulkner has given us and rearranging its episodes chronologically to understand it more fully leaves us with three questions: (1) Does such a willful and radical reconstruction make the work another novel and so prevent the reading experience Faulkner wished us to have? (2) Is there an ascertainable reason for Faulkner's achronological presentation? and (3) What is gained by reading the novel in the way we just have? These are legitimate and fundamental questions to raise about all of Faulkner's writing, but they are particularly relevant to *Go Down, Moses.*

No modern American novelist is more aware of the forces of history than Faulkner, or more insistent that we remain consciously aware of them. No modern American novelist is more aware of our need to make meaning out of ruptured memory and disjunctive episodes of the past than Faulkner, or more aware of how our minds always search for sequences in order to explain things. The novel to which *Go Down, Moses* is most clearly related, *Absalom, Absalom!*, makes just such ideas basic: all six points of view in that novel—those of Rosa Coldfield, General Compson, Mr. Compson, Thomas Sutpen, Quentin, and Shreve—keep going over the facts of Thomas Sutpen's life chronologically, under the premise (correct, as it turns out) that only an accurate sequence of all the facts that can be known (and, when the need arises, surmised) can unfold the significance of Sutpen's life—not only its meaning for Sutpen but its meaning for those who follow him.

At the same time that this understanding governs Faulkner's fiction, he is also deeply aware that none of us ever has all of the facts at any time: that life is full of surmises, guesses, and reexaminations and that any investigation, like any story, is only as good as the reliability and insight of the narrator. Faulkner's own deep attraction to the mystery novel as a form—seen in his own work, from *Sanctuary* to *Intruder in the Dust, Knight's Gambit,* and *Requiem for a Nun*—illustrates that the fiction writer's art is the art of investigation—of solving the puzzling, the yet unknown, the unexplained—so that all of us, reading fiction, write it too. This is one of the glorious truths about fiction, not a shortcoming: Faulkner expects and invites our collaboration and our complicity, and to ensure it, he gives us fragments of a story so that we, like his characters, must go over and over them to make sense of them. When the various descendants of the McCaslin-Beauchamp-Edmonds family keep recalling their own ancestry and the network of family relations they possess and that possesses them, we see inside the novel what we, outside it, are also doing. Faulkner wanted and expected his work to be read and reread, because only on rereadings will all the relationships, analogies, and recollections and misrecollections appear that could not if there were one single, over-riding presentation and plot.

This is true throughout Faulkner's career; even *Soldiers' Pay* and *Flags in the Dust*, as largely sequential as they are, come to us episodi-cally and repay second and third readings. Peter Brooks has aligned these characteristics of Faulkner with current critical theory in remarks about *Absalom, Absalom!* that apply equally well to *Go Down, Moses*:

> The actions and sequences of action of the narrative are struc-tured into larger wholes by the play of enigma and solutions: the hermeneutic acts as a large, shaping force, allowing us to sort out, to group, to see the significance of actions, to rename their sequences in terms of their significance for the narrative as a whole. We read in the suspense created by the hermeneutic code, structuring actions according to its indications, restructuring as we move through partial revelations and misleading clues, moving toward the fullness of meaning. At the end, with what Barthes describes as a full "saturation" of the matrix of the sentence—now fully predicated—we are in a position to gain retrospective under-standing of the whole.[48]

Rereading a work chronologically is one of the ways we move "toward the fullness of meaning." But in *Go Down, Moses* the need and the reason for partial and incomplete fragments has further point than the faltering of knowledge, memory, or hearsay and legend: in this novel they reflect and illustrate the ways in which such powerful forces as race and racism cause characters to distort, repress, or conceal the story of past and present events in which they are involved.

Furthermore, in a culture in which something like race is direc-tional and decisive, but not always known (e.g., for a long time Ike does not know about L. Q. C. McCaslin's relationship with Eunice, though he has premonitions long before he works out the facts by reading commissary ledgers) characters must learn to live with approx-imations—with oral tradition, legend, partial truths, family tradition, their own best judgments. Just as "Pantaloon in Black" forces us into the position of a victimized black and a victimized redneck suffering from opposite sides, so the novel forces us to question each character, each act, each expression as redolent of deeper meanings—meanings that change as we change perspectives. Rendering *Go Down, Moses* chronological, as we have done here, is one sure way of cracking open the ruptures and bringing together distant or repetitive episodes. Reading thus against the grain—especially if we also read chronologically, with the grain—makes the novel even richer.

We can now see more forcefully that reconstructed chronologically, *Go Down, Moses* discloses on every page Faulkner's observations on the legacies and conditions of race that are so fundamental to understanding Yoknapatawpha and Jefferson in 1940 and 1941 and are no less true today.

I began work on this book by living for the month of January 1993 in Oxford, Mississippi, where a number of residents taught me about Faulkner's culture, past and present. One noon, when taking my regular dinner in the town's central restaurant for residents, located just a door or two south of the square, I noticed a certain uneasiness among the staff and some of my other friends there. Finally, one of them ventured to ask me if I had yet seen the *USA Today* weekend edition that had just come out. I hadn't. They fell silent. Later, I bought a copy. What they had seen was the single story under "Mississippi" for the weekend; it was about one man attacking another with a razor for reasons unknown and nearly killing his victim. No person was identified by race, but the implications were clear enough. *Will it never end?* I could hear friends of mine saying; will the national press forever see *this* as the sole way to portray Mississippi?

Wounded myself, I found that such stories seemed to follow work on this book. During the spring of 1993, when I was teaching an undergraduate seminar on Faulkner at the University of Massachusetts, Amherst, the *New York Times* published a story on a young Mississippi high-school graduate, a black man, who had been arrested for driving without a license and was later found hanged by the shoestring of his sneaker in his cell. His parents said he would never take his own life, because he had too many plans for the future. The *Times* noted that sixteen similar incidents had occurred previous to this one in the past year. In the summer of 1993, while drafting this book in Cortland,

New York, I read, again in the *New York Times*, of Jonestown, Mississippi, where unemployment and poverty had forced mobile whites to leave and where only immobile blacks remain. Jonestown is now a ghetto where, in the population of 1,476, only 100 persons have jobs. Now, proofreading this book once more in Cortland early in 1996, I read of a neighbor from Amherst researching a 30-year-old murder case of a black man whose Hattiesburg, Mississippi, home was allegedly firebombed by the Ku Klux Klan; it is a case Carl Vigeland hopes to solve. Such crushing circumstances were daily reminders to Faulkner, too, as he scrutinized the Mississippi of his day for his fiction.

But the South is not alone. Five days before the story on Jonestown appeared, I read of eight white supremacists who were being held in Los Angeles on charges of preparing to blow up one of the largest black churches, which had attempted to do neighborhood rehabilitation after the trial of Rodney King; these men had additional plans to kill King himself. In August 1993, as I wrote the conclusion to this book, I read of the trial of two white men who were charged with abducting a black tourist from Brooklyn while he was buying a newspaper at a shopping plaza near Tampa, Florida, taking him to a remote field, showering him with gasoline, and setting him afire simply because he was black. And in Auburn, New York, less than 50 miles from where I was sitting, white supremacists, in conjunction with members of the Ku Klux Klan, were planning a march through the main streets of town to demonstrate white superiority and to ask for the elimination of blacks from their city. Now, in January 1996, black churches are being burned to the ground in neighboring Alabama. *Will it never end?*

We are sophisticated enough today—or perhaps *hardened* is the right word—that such events are made public. This was not so true in 1940, and in Mississippi, where feelings were just as strong. That meant that racial conditions were a good deal more sensitive than we might suppose, and attitudes toward race were as conflicted and complex and problematic as we could possibly imagine. Part of Faulkner's historical importance as a Southern novelist was that he, following in the wake of the black novelist Richard Wright, made race a central factor in his work. But he did so with humanity, caution, and delicacy. One of the basic reasons Faulkner's work is not more explicit is that the matters he chooses to portray are themselves clouded, bewildering, and only imperfectly recognized or known. It is understandable that Ike McCaslin, who learned things quickly and well and was as observant as many in his time, did not know of the miscegenation in his family's past and, when he learned it, had no clear tradition to follow in responding to it. There is an extraordinary courage in his act, at the age of 16, of opening those family ledgers to learn the truth about his own ancestry, especially with the premonitions he had; and there is an extraordinary truth in the fact that he was somehow born with those premonitions. It is an extraordinary revelation of Rider's psyche that in attempting to confront the cause of Mannie's unexplained death, he pursues all those situations in his life in which he too has been a victim, and that all those situations involve his sense of racial division. There is something painfully accurate about the white deputy whose own feelings so outpace his understanding and his language that he seems to talk at times incoherently or in clichés, when in fact his monologue is full of self-revelation, through which he rapidly matures.

All of these moments in *Go Down, Moses* insist that the lives of whites and blacks in Yoknapatawpha are inseparable, indivisible. As Philip M. Weinstein has memorably put it, "Bound to each other through seven generations that begin and end with miscegenation, the blacks see in the whites the conditions they cannot escape, the whites see in the blacks the guilt they cannot assuage."[49] Faulkner worried about this deeply and always by 1940. Eighteen years later, on February 20, 1958, he would tell those at a conference at the University of Virginia, "It is possible that the white race and the Negro race can never really like and trust the other; this for the reason that the white man can never really know the Negro, because the white man has forced the Negro to be always a Negro rather than another human being in their dealings, and therefore the Negro cannot afford, does not dare, to be open with the white man and let the white man know what he, the Negro thinks" (quoted in Peavy, 64). Faulkner had already shown intimations of that nearly everywhere in *Go Down, Moses*, yet the tragedy continued, and he continued to talk about it.

Eric J. Sundquist thinks that "*Go Down, Moses* may be Faulkner's most honest and personally revealing novel" (153), and various documents, including sources cited here and others listed in the bibliography, demonstrate that this is surely so (although they can also show Faulkner surrendering at times to rigidity under danger and pressure, and even a kind of cynicism). Yet this honesty does have its rewards, evident in Faulkner's frequently unblinking portrayal of Yoknapatawpha under siege and in his penetration and prescience concerning racism in the South. Through Gavin Stevens, he shows us the possible limitations of the well-intentioned, well-meaning liberal: smugness, ineptitude, blindness, too-easy generalizing, too-easy optimism. Beside Gavin, he places Roth, Molly, and an unnamed redneck, all of whose own immediate contributions to the alleviation of racial tension in Yoknapatawpha—if feeble, short-lived, and more restricted—are nevertheless, potentially or by way of illustration, more beneficial over time and with repeated effort.

These limited gestures were behavioral models for Faulkner in 1942, and he used his fiction to render them unforgettable not only to the South but also to his country at large. At that time, they had small chance of succeeding very dramatically or very soon, but they would have had a slimmer chance yet if presented chronologically—and thus more openly and forcefully. The miscegenation of time thus both concedes—and reveals—the fractured South it portrays so dramatically. Faulkner could have written this honestly in no other way than indirectly. The question *Go Down, Moses* most pronouncedly asks us in the 1990s is whether we can, even now, respond to anything more pointedly put or understood—and, if and when we do, what form our own responses may take.

APPENDICES

Appendix I:
A Chronology of Go Down, Moses

(This chronology, originally published as part of an essay by Meredith Smith in Mississippi Quarterly *36:3 [Summer 1983]: 319–28, has been supplemented and slightly revised by Arthur F. Kinney. Conjectural dates are in parentheses. Many dates are contradicted by others also in the text or are inferred; in such instances, Smith gives the reasoning behind her choices, and her essay should be consulted for any further study.)*

1772	Lucius Quintus Carothers McCaslin born in Carolina.
1779	Thucydus born to Roskus and Fibby.
(1797–1799)	Twin boys (Amodeus/Buddy and Theophilus/Buck) born to L. Q. C. McCaslin and wife.
1807	L. Q. C. McCaslin buys Eunice.
1809	Eunice married to Thucydus; Sam Fathers born.
1810	Tomasina ("Tomy," "Tomey") born to Eunice.
(1812–1814)	Hubert Beauchamp born; "Warwick" built by Hubert's father; L. Q. C. McCaslin's wife dies.
1830	Percival Brownlee born.
1832	Eunice drowns 25 December.
1833	Tomey's Terrell (Turl) born to Tomey in June; Tomey dies.
1837	L. Q. C. McCaslin dies 27 June; Roskus and Fibby freed same day.
1838	Tennie born.
1841	Roskus dies 12 January; Thucydus leaves McCaslin plantation 3 November; Thucydus sets up blacksmith shop in Jefferson in December.

1843	Boon Hogganbeck born.
1849	Fibby dies 1 August.
1850	McCaslin Edmonds (Cass) born.
Early 1850s	Buck and Buddy establish $1,000 legacy for Tomey's Turl.
1854	Thucydus dies 17 February. Tomey's Turl is 21 in June; elects to stay on plantation.
1856	Uncle Buck buys Percival Brownlee on 3 March; Brownlee freed 2 October.
1859	During summer, Uncle Buddy wins Tennie in poker game; she marries Tomey's Turl. Amodeus McCaslin Beauchamp, son of Tomey's Turl and Tennie, is born and dies in winter.
1861	Civil War begins; Uncle Buck joins John Sartoris's regiment.
1862	Percival Brownlee reappears as preacher; daughter of Tomey's Turl and Tennie born, dies.
1863	Uncle Buck rides in and out of Gayoso Hotel, Memphis, while it is held by Yankee troops; Tomey's Turl and Tennie have third child, who dies.
(1864)	Cass Edmonds orphaned (possibly earlier). James Beauchamp (Tennie's Jim) born to Tomey's Turl and Tennie 29 December.
1865	Uncle Buck returns from war.
(1865–1866)	Uncle Buck and Sophonsiba Beauchamp married.
1866	Percival Brownlee reappears; seen by Uncle Buck.
1867	Isaac McCaslin born in October; two weeks later, Hubert Beauchamp, Isaac's uncle, seals gold pieces in cup.
1869	Fonsiba (named for Sophonsiba Beauchamp) born to Tomey's Turl and Tennie in early June.
1870	Uncle Buddy dies; later, Uncle Buck dies; Cass takes over McCaslin plantation.
(1871–1873)	Sophonsiba discovers Uncle Hubert's "cook" and forces him to dismiss her.
1873	Uncle Hubert removes last gold piece from cup and replaces cup 19 January.
(1873–1877)	"Warwick" burns; Uncle Hubert and Tennie's great-grand-father move to McCaslin plantation.
1874	Lucius Beauchamp (named for L. Q. C. McCaslin; later changes name to Lucas) born 17 March to Tomey's Turl and Tennie.
1875	Isaac shoots rabbit.

Appendix I

(1874–1875)	Zack Edmonds born.
(1876–1877)	Uncle Hubert dies.
(1877)	Sophonsiba Beauchamp McCaslin dies (possibly earlier).
1877	In March Jobaker dies on McCaslin plantation; Sam Fathers goes to live in hunting cabin in Big Bottom. Ike goes on first deer hunt in November. Ike receives gun from Cass (his first cousin) 25 December.
(1877–1878)	Ike and Boon buy a wild pony when Ike is 10 years old.
1878	Ike tries to see Old Ben in June; finally succeeds.
1879	Boon shoots black. In November Ike kills first buck; Ash goes hunting; Walt Ewall shoots buck from caboose of logging train; Ike and Cass discuss mortality and immortality.
1880	Ike kills first bear in November.
1881	In summer Ike and Fyce corner Old Ben; Sam captures Lion after doe, fawn, and colt killed; Cass and Ike discuss truth. Lion participates in hunt for Old Ben in November; strangers watch; Boon sleeps with Lion.
1882	Hunters corner Old Ben in November; General Compson draws blood.
1883	In December Ike and Boon go to Memphis; Boon and Lion kill Old Ben; Lion dies; Ike stays on with Sam and Boon; Sam dies.
1883–1884	In winter Ike reads ledgers of McCaslin plantation; hunters incorporate and lease hunting rights on new land.
1884	Hunters go farther into woods to hunt in November.
1885	Boon made town marshal of Hoke's in January. Major DeSpain leases timber rights on Big Woods in spring. Ike revisits Big Woods in summer; sees snake and Boon. Tennie's Jim disappears (forever) on 29 December, the night he turns 21; Ike follows him to Jackson with his third of legacy ($1,000) but fails to find him.
1886	Ike returns to plantation 12 January. Cass learns Percival Brownlee runs a brothel. Fonsiba married in July, with Cass's permission; she and her husband leave the plantation. Ike finds Fonsiba and her husband on a desolate farm outside Midnight, Arkansas, on 11 December; they refuse $1,000 legacy, but Ike leaves it for them in a local bank.
1887	Tomey's Turl dies on McCaslin plantation.
1888	In October Ike turns 21; he discusses family ledgers with Cass in plantation commissary; he unseals Hubert's legacy; Ike

	leaves plantation for bungalow in Jefferson; Cass brings Ike money and forces him to accept a loan in lieu of legacy or income from plantation.
1889	Ike becomes carpenter in October; unable to repay loan due Cass.
(1889–1890)	Ike marries wife (unnamed).
1895	Lucas turns 21 on 17 March; claims $1,000 inheritance; Lucas marries Molly (sometime between 17 March 1895 and 17 March 1896).
(1890–1897)	Cass Edmonds dies; Zack takes over plantation.
1897–1898	Henry born to Lucas and Molly in winter.
1898	Carothers (Roth) Edmonds (like Lucas, named after L. Q. C. McCaslin) born in March to Zack; his mother dies in childbirth. Lucas and Zack fight in autumn.
(1898)	Tennie Beauchamp dies (possibly later).
1905	In summer Roth Edmonds rejects Henry Beauchamp by taking bed for himself and making Henry sleep on pallet.
1917	George Wilkins born.
(1917–1918)	Roth Edmonds fights in World War I.
1921	Zack Edmonds dies; Roth inherits plantation; Lucas sets up still.
1923	Nat born to Lucas and Molly in spring.
(1937)	Ike's wife dies (possibly earlier).
1939	Roth meets James Beauchamp's granddaughter in November.
1940	Roth takes James Beauchamp's granddaughter to New Mexico for two weeks in January. In July Samuel Worsham Beauchamp ("Butch") executed in Chicago; brought to Jefferson for burial, at request of his grandmother Molly and Miss Belle Worsham, and with support of Gavin Stevens and local newspaper editor Wilmoth. George Wilkins and Nat Beauchamp secretly married in October (or forge marriage document with this date); Roth's child by James Beauchamp's granddaughter born. In November Ike hunts with Roth; James Beauchamp's granddaughter arrives with son and is rejected by Roth and Ike.
1941	Rider and Mannie married in February. In spring Lucas Beauchamp and George Wilkins caught (by sheriff) with illegal stills and tried. George buys new still with money from Lucas in summer. In August Mannie dies; Rider is lynched; unnamed salesman offers Lucas gold-divining machine; Molly seeks

divorce. In September or October Molly takes machine from Lucas; she and Lucas go to court for divorce proceedings; Lucas changes mind; divorce proceedings canceled.

1942   George and Nat expect child in spring.

Appendix II:
Published Accounts of
Lynchings in Mississippi

A. Nelse Patton (1908)

(The following two accounts of the lynching of Nelse Patton were transcribed by Arthur F. Kinney. An earlier transcription of the first account, with minor errors, can be found in John B. Cullen in collaborations with Floyd C. Watkins, Old Times in the Faulkner Country *[Chapel Hill, N.C.: University of North Carolina Press, 1961], 93–98.)*

From the Lafayette County Press, *9 September 1908 (Oxford, Mississippi).*

NEGRO BRUTE CUTS WOMAN'S THROAT

MRS. MATTIE McMULLEN, A WHITE WOMAN THE VICTIM—LIVED BUT TEN MINUTES AFTER THE TRAGEDY. SHERIFF HARTSFIELD AND POSSE OF CITIZENS GIVE CHASE AND LAND NEGRO IN JAIL

MOB STORMS JAIL AND KILLS DESPERADO

Officers and Guards Overpowered, and Failing to Find the Keys the Orderly Mob Quietly and Deliberately Took Matters in Their

Own Hands, Forced Entrance to Cell Where Negro Was Confined
Negro Armed with Poker Puts Up Desperate Fight and Is Killed.

One of the coldest blooded murders and most brutal crimes known
to the criminal calendar was perpetrated one mile north of town yester-
day morning about ten o'clock, when a black brute of unsavory reputation by the name of Nelse Patton attacked Mrs. Mattie McMullen, a
respected white woman, with a razor, cutting her throat from ear to ear
and causing almost instant death. Reports as to the cause of the tragedy
vary, but as near as can be learned the particulars are these:

Mrs. McMullen, whose husband was confined at the time in the
county jail at this place, was a hard working woman living alone with
her 17-year-old daughter and two other very small children. It seems
that Mr. McMullen wanted to communicate with his wife, and as was
his custom at such occasions, he called the murderer, who was a
"trusty" prisoner at the jail, to carry the missive. Arriving at the house,
the negro, who was in an intoxicated condition, walked into the house
without knocking and took a seat. Seeing the woman apparently alone
and without protection, his animal passion was aroused and he made
insulting remarks to her. He was ordered from the house and some
angry words passed between them, when the woman started toward
the bureau drawer to get her pistol. The brute seeing her design made
a rush at the woman from behind and drawing the razor cut her throat
from ear to ear, almost severing the head from the body. The dying
woman rushed out of the house, and the daughter hearing the confu-
sion rushed in, and was instantly grabbed by the negro. Jerking herself
from the brute's grasp, she followed her mother who had fallen dead a
few yards from the house. The daughter's screams alarmed the neighbors who quickly responded to the call and immediately sent in a hurried telephone message to the Press office to summon officers and a
physician, who in less than twenty minutes were on the way to the
scene of the murder. The news spread like wild fire and it was but a
short while until the sheriff was joined by a posse of citizens all in hot
and close pursuit of the brute. After chasing the negro three or four
miles over fences, through briars and fields he suddenly ran amuck of
Johnny Cullen, the 14-year-old son of Lin Cullen, who was out with a
double-barreled shotgun. Seeing the negro coming towards him, he

called a halt, but the negro paid no attention to the command and the boy let him have a load of No. 5 shot in the chest, which slackened his speed but did not stop him. The boy gave him another charge in the left arm and side which stopped him. The negro was at once surrounded by his pursuers and gladly gave up. Over a hundred shots were fired from all kinds of weapons but the negro was out of range. Being weak from loss of blood, the brute was put on a horse and hurried to jail.

As soon as the news spread of the capture, hundreds of people began to gather around the jail and in small groups about the street. They were not indulging in idle threats, but from the seriousness of their expression one could see the negro's fate was sealed.

Between nine and ten o'clock the crowd began swelling to large proportions about the jail. Speeches were made advocating letting the law take its course and vice-versa, but patience had fallen far short of being a virtue in a crowd like that. One wild shout went up, with a rush the crowd advanced on the jail, pushing open doors and jumping through windows. Officers and guards were overpowered and disarmed. The keys could not be found, but the hardware stores and blacksmith shops were made to furnish the necessary tools and a set of quiet and determined men plied them. Four and one-half hours of hard and persistent work it took to break through the thick walls of steel and masonry. The hall was at last reached, and a search of the cell occupied by that black fiend incarnate was made. It was at last found and broken into. Crouched and cringing in a dark corner of the cell, with the gleam of murder in his eye, stood the miserable wretch armed with an iron poker awaiting the advance. In one, two, three order the mob entered the cell, and in the same order the iron descended upon their heads, blood flew, the negro having all the advantage in his dark corner, held the crowd at bay and refused to come out. Only one thing was left to do. It was done. 26 pistol shots vibrated throughout the corridors of the solid old jail, and when the smoke cleared away the limp and lifeless body of the brute told the story.

The body was hustled down stairs to terra-firma, the rope was produced, the hangman's noose properly adjusted about the neck, and the drag to the court house yard began.

This morning the passerby saw the lifeless body of a negro suspended from a tree—it told the tale, that the murder of a white woman had been avenged—the public had done their duty. Following is the verdict of the Coroner's Jury:

We the Coroners Jury of inquest impaneled and sworn to investigate the death of Nelse Patton, colored, find after inspecting the body and examining necessary witnesses that to the best of our knowledge and belief, the said Nelse Patton came to his death from gunshot or pistol wounds inflicted by parties to us unknown. That any one of a number of wounds would have been sufficient to cause death. We find further that Sheriff J. C. Hartsfield and his deputies were diligent in their efforts to protect said Nelse Patton from the time of his arrest until they were overpowered by a mob of several hundred men who stormed the jail and dug their way through the walls until they reached the cell in which said Nelse Patton was confined and that said officers never surrendered the keys of jail or cells but that the locks were forced by some party or parties to us unknown and that the said Nelse Patton was shot with pistols or guns while in his cell and while attempting to protect himself with an iron rod. We further find that said Nelse Patton was dead before being brought from the jail and being hung.

Respectfully submitted,
E. O. Davidson
R. S. Adams
P. E. Matthews
B. P. Gray
A. F. Calloway
F. Wood

From the Jackson, Mississippi, Daily Clarion-Ledger, *Thursday, 10 September 1908.*

SULLIVAN'S HOT TALK ON OXFORD LYNCHING

FORMER UNITED STATES SENATOR FROM MISSISSIPPI LED THE MOB

(Associated Press Report)

Memphis, Tenn., Sept. 9.—A special from Oxford, Miss., quotes former U.S. Senator W. V. Sullivan as follows, with reference to the lynching of last night:

"I led the mob which lynched Nelse Patton and I am proud of it.

"I directed every movement of the mob, and I did everything I could to see that he was lynched.

"Cut a white woman's throat? and a negro? Of course I wanted him lynched.

"I saw his body dangling from a tree this morning and I am glad of it.

"When I heard of the horrible crime, I started to work immediately to get a mob. I did all I could to raise one. I was at the jail last night and I heard Judge Roane advise against lynching. I got up immediately after and urged the mob to lynch Patton.

"I aroused the mob and directed them to storm the jail.

"I had my revolver, but did not use it. I gave it to a deputy sheriff and told him: 'Shoot Patton and shoot to kill.'

"He used the revolver and shot. I suppose the bullets from my gun were some of those that killed the negro.

"I don't care what investigation is made, or what are the consequences. I am willing to stand them.

"I wouldn't mind standing the consequences any time for lynching a man who cut a white woman's throat. I will lead a mob in such a case any time."

B. Elwood Higginbotham (1935)

Of the following eight accounts of the lynching of Elwood Higginbotham, the first five (all from the Oxford, Mississippi, Eagle, which was a weekly newspaper in 1935) were transcribed by Frank Childrey, Jr., and Arthur F. Kinney. The last three were transcribed by Kinney.

Appendix II

From the Oxford, Mississippi, Eagle, *29 August 1935, p.1, col.2; p.4, col.5*

JURORS DRAWN FOR SEPTEMBER TERM

Selections Being Notified of Jury Duty for
September Term of Circuit Court Starting 9th

The circuit clerk, sheriff, and chancery clerk have drawn the list of jurors to serve for the first week of September term of the circuit court to get under way September 9 with Judge Taylor H. McElroy presiding.

There are some eight or ten criminal cases and about twice that many civil cases listed for attention of the circuit court and likely several other cases will be docketed before the term starts. The most noted or notorious case is that of Jesse Tatum held on two charges, one for arson and the other for murder.

The grand jury will also consider the plight of Elwood Higginbotham, negro slayer of Glen D. Roberts. The negro has been in the Hinds county jail every [*sic*] since his capture in Pontotoc county about three months ago.

The following will make up the jury for the September term:

Beat 1—Posey Franklin, Douglas Walker, Ed Dooley, Buster Littlejohn, Hulett Johnson, Jess Anderson, George Young, Jim Blasengame, Elco McClarty, Curt Mize.

Beat 2—Toy Duncan, U. G. Smith, John Jordan, Erle Sparks, B. G. Coffey, J. J. Littlejohn, W. E. Ferrell, Mack Parks, Ed Stone, Menken Sneed.

Beat 3—Jesse Smith, Lon Weaver, L. L. Hargrove, J. R. Sullender, J. A. Lewis, J. A. Wolfe, Frank Smith, W. P. Haley, G. C. Landreth, R. L. Young.

Beat 4—L. V. Gray, C. A. Martin, John A. Cooper, E. H. Byers, Fred Higginbotham, J. H. Cannon, Hugh Carothers, R. X. Williams, P. D. Ayles, Dud S. Foust.

Beat 5—A. S. Cooper, R. R. Sockwell, C. B. Davis, C. P. Hall, W. E. Brown, D. D. Oswalt, R. H. Morrison, Dewey McClarty, J. W. Gault, Lee J. Garrison.

From the Oxford, Mississippi, Eagle, 12 September 1935, p. 1, cols. 3–4.

JESSE TATUM'S MURDER TRIAL FRIDAY; HIGGINBOTHAM'S IS SET FOR MONDAY

Elwood Higginbotham, Negro, Brought from Jackson Jail, Pleads Not Guilty to Murder Charge

Elwood Higginbotham, confessed negro murder [*sic*] of Glen D. Roberts, pleaded not guilty to the charge of first degree murder Tuesday and will face trial Monday of next week. A special venire of 50 Lafayette county citizens has been drawn for jury duty in the case.

The court appointed L. C. Hutton, local attorney, to represent the negro in the case.

Glen Roberts, well known and popular Lafayette county farmer, was killed on the night of Monday, May 21st. A discharge from a shotgun in the hands of the negro brought almost instant death.

After the killing, the negro eluded posses for two days and night [*sic*], finally being captured near Pontotoc from whence he was taken to the Hinds county jail at Jackson where he stayed until brought to Oxford the first of the week for trial.

From the Oxford, Mississippi, Eagle, 19 September 1935, p. 1, col. 3.

COURT ENDS AFTER 9 DAYS

Longest Term in Years, Murder Trials Consuming Most of Time; Several Minor Cases Settled

Circuit court, in session nine days, closed court Wednesday evening. This was the longest term of court held during the past four years. The Tatum and Higginbotham murder trials accounted for the greatest part of the time. . . .

Appendix II

From the Oxford, Mississippi, Eagle, *19 September 1935, p. 1, col. 7;
p. 4, col. 3.*

LIFE IMPRISONMENT FOR TATUM;
MOB LYNCHES HIGGINBOTHAM NEGRO

Career of Negro Who Killed Glen Roberts Terminates
at the End of a Rope Tuesday Night

Mob law walked in Lafayette county Tuesday night.

Judge Lynch passed sentence: "Hanged by the neck until dead"
on the person of Elwood Higginbotham, confessed negro murderer of
Glen D. Roberts. The black man was hanged by a mob of about 75
men just north of Three-Way, on the old Russell road, about 9 o'clock
Tuesday night.

Mr. Roberts was killed by the discharge from a shotgun in the
hands of the negro on the night of Monday, May 21st.

The case against the negro for murder went to trial Tuesday
morning and was given to the jury that evening. The jury was still out,
disagreeing, when the hanging took place.

Rumors that the jury stood 10 for conviction with 2 for acquittal
were said to have incited the mob.

Entirely Unexpected

The mob action came as a complete surprise to all the court officials. The negro was in Oxford for one day last week and was brought
back for trial Tuesday morning. During that time no demonstration of
any kind was made.

A crowd of approximately 75 men, with faces smudged with dirt
to prevent identification, converged on the jail about 8:30 o'clock.
Jailer Pritchard and three deputies were unable to reason with the
determined white men.

The attack was evidently well planned and went off with little
noise of any kind. The jail telephone wires were out. The mobsters
quickly searched the jail until the keys were found and then broke into
the cell block. A messenger was hurriedly sent for Sheriff S. T. Lyles

who arrived at the jail just as the mob was leaving with the prisoner. His attempts to stop the men were futile. He was overpowered by the mob members who held him until fellow mobsters carried the negro off to his death.

Prisoners Attempt Escape

As the door to the cell block was unlocked by the mob, two desperate federal prisoners, Claude Lott and Wilton Smith, made an attempt to escape by running down the stairs but were captured and returned to their cells by the mob.

Court was still in session, with court officials present, waiting for the jury to come in when word reached town that there was no need of any further court action in the case of state versus Elwood Higginbotham, negro.

From Oxford, Mississippi, Eagle, *3 October 1935, p. 1, col. 2.*

AROUND THE COURT HOUSE
SIMPLE AND QUIET

Outside of a few negroes stealing horses and shooting craps, the "simple have been very quiet" this week, said Justice Bennett. It sounded as if the justice meant that only the simple violated the law and were yanked up in his court. However, he probably meant that only the simple get caught.

From New York City Daily Worker, *24 September 1935.*

ELWOOD HIGGINBOTHAM—HERO OF SHARE-
CROPPERS—VICTIM OF LYNCH MOB

On Wednesday, Sept. 18. Elwood Higgenbotham [*sic*], a 28-year-old Negro sharecropper, was lynched by a mob at Oxford, Mississippi, while a Circuit Court all-white jury was "deliberating" at his trial for the "murder" of Glen Roberts, a white landlord.

The local press reported that "a restless crowd, estimated to number 100 to 150 men, stormed the jail, dragged the prisoner out of his cell and whisked him out to the country where his screaming pleas for mercy were refused and he was hanged to a tree beside a lonely, wooded road."

Official whitewash of the lynchers followed promptly. Circuit Court Judge McElroy, in whose court the "trial" took place, stated that Sheriff S. T. Lyles had told him that none of the mob was recognized either by the sheriff, his deputies or the jailer from whom they had obtained the keys to the prison "by force."

Was Leader of Union

"Sheriff Lyles told me the men were masked and could not be identified, so I don't suppose there is anything that can be done right now," Judge McElroy said. He "indicated" that the matter "might be referred" to the County Grand Jury "when it meets several months hence."

Higgenbotham was one of the leaders of the Share Croppers Union in Oxford and had long been singled out by the landlords. The "excuse" for the mob assault and lynching of this heroic worker goes back to another unsuccessful effort to murder him some months ago.

Higgenbotham had a field cultivated through which landlords tried to cut a short road. Higgenbotham fenced off the field to save it from destruction. This move immediately put him into the class of "uppity niggers" in the language of the arrogant landlord class.

Soon after this short cut was blocked off, Roberts, a white landlord, organized a lynch mob against Higgenbotham. A native white worker, and Communist Party leader in Oxford, wrote at that time of the events of the succeeding two murderous days and nights, and of the final capture and jailing of Higgenbotham.

Tells of Lynch Attempt

The letter states: "Tuesday night a mob of at least 25 white farmers armed with pistols went to Higgenbotham's house. Higgenbotham, his wife and three children had gone to bed and were awakened by Tom Likkings demanding of him that he open the door and come out. Now, Glen Roberts with pistol in hand forced his way into the house. Higgenbotham who didn't have time to dress ran and when Roberts started after him Higgenbotham shot him down with a Winchester.

"When the mob of white lynchers on the outside heard the shot, they became so frightened that they left the lynch leader to his own fate and sent to town to get the law to come. Now started one of the typical manhunts with bloodhounds and the mob, armed to the teeth rushing through the woods, hills and swamps. Infuriated over the failure to capture Higgenbotham, Oxford's "finest" with the officers of the law leading them on, started to hunt up his family.

Sister Is Beaten

"A brother-in-law was dragged out of bed and lodged in jail without any charges against him, and released only a week after on bond and told to get out of town at once. Higgenbotham's sister was beaten so mercilessly by a mob while officers looked on until her clothes in tatters was [sic] mangled in with her flesh and blood. The mob also hunted his brothers with the intention of burning them in the father's front yard should they fail to find and lynch Higgenbotham. Whenever kinfolk of Higgenbotham's could be found the armed mob fell over them like maddened hyenas, bent on murder.

"The boys in the C.C.C. campus nearby were recruited for the murderous manhunt.

Hunted in Swamp

"The second day after spending most of the day in the swamp in water, sometimes to his very neck, tired and hungry, not having a bit to eat and no clothes, having had to jump out of bed and run for his life, wounded and torn by briars, Higgenbotham was found by officers in an adjoining county unable to get out of the water. The fact that he was caught in another county is the only explanation for Higgenbotham being here yet. He was rushed to Jackson, Miss., for safekeeping. . . ."

This wanton murder of an innocent Negro sharecropper has aroused a tremendous anger among many Southern workers. At the same time the heroic struggle that Higgenbotham put up to save his life stands as another milestone in the blood-covered road to final emancipation.

The Mississippi white worker concludes his letter with the deep pledge of intensified working class loyalty, and of Higgenbotham he writes:

"There runs through this horrible two day man-hunt a thread of glorious and heroic self-defense of one single Negro with no clothes on and nothing to eat for two days and nights defending himself with a rifle against a maddened horde, running into the hundreds of the most lawless characters, armed with the finest high powered rifles to be had. The Negro workers of the South have reason to look with confidence to the coming struggle for power, while the white landlords have just as much reason to think about the same struggle with fear and despair. And we white workers should feel proud of our Negro brothers."

(Author's note: The Daily Worker *was an official publication of the United States Communist Party.)*

From the Spartanburg, South Carolina, Herald, *19 September 1935.*

ANOTHER LYNCHING

Mississippi records another lynching. This time it followed the disagreement of a jury and the defendant was taken from jail and hanged after the jury was dismissed by the presiding judge.

The state of Mississippi will come in for justifiable criticism for not making an effort to protect this prisoner. No matter how heinous the crime of which he was charged may have been the defendant was in the hands of the authorities and it seems they made no effort to protect him.

The case is more to be criticized because the negro defendant had been tried by a jury of white men and in the face of infuriated public opinion. Failure to reach a verdict under such circumstances would indicate that there was no excuse for a body of 150 [*sic*] men to raid the jail, and execute the man whom a jury refused to convict. Incidents like this are the cause of agitation for a federal anti-lynching law.

From the Charlotte, North Carolina, Observer, 22 September 1935.

LYNCHED DURING TRIAL

After his trial in court on a murder charge had gone to the jury and while the jury still was deliberating, Ellwood [*sic*] Higginbotham, negro, was lynched late Tuesday night by a mob estimated by officers at 150 to 200 men, which stormed the jail at Oxford, Miss.

The negro was charged with having slain Glen Roberts, a white planter, in "cold blood," last May.

The mob broke down the jail doors and seized the negro, took him to a lonely side road a few miles from town and almost within sight of the State university, and hanged him.

When Judge Taylor McElroy was officially informed of the lynching, he called the jury into court and dismissed it.

(Author's note: Actually, Higginbotham was taken to a black residential area just northeast of town and away from the University campus, which is to the west of town. I am grateful to the nation's most comprehensive archive on affairs dealing with lynching throughout the country, located at the library of the Tuskegee Institute in Alabama.)

Appendix III:
Interview with Russell Warren Howe

New York, February 27, 1956

William Faulkner said in an exclusive interview this week that he believed there was a grave danger of civil war in the South.

The Nobel Prizewinning author, who runs a cotton plantation near Oxford, Mississippi, the state where tension runs highest, said he had "always been on the side of the Negroes" but that if shooting started he would "fight for Mississippi against the United States."

Commenting on the incidents which have made the battle for Negro equality the main home affairs issue in the 1956 presidential election campaign, Faulkner said:

"The Northerner doesn't understand what's going on down there. He doesn't realize that most people in Alabama, Mississippi or Tennessee will go to any lengths. They will even accept another civil war. If the National Association for the Advancement of Colored People and the liberal opposition push this thing, the South will go to its guns.

"The NAACP have done a very fine job. Now they should stop. They have got us off balance. They should let us try to regain balance, not put us in a position that makes us feel like an underdog with regard to the rest of America.

"My position is this. My people owned slaves and the very obligation we have to take care of these people is morally bad. It is a position which is completely untenable. But I would wish now that the liberals would stop—they should let us sweat in our own fears for a little while. If we are pushed by the government we shall become an underdog people fighting back because we can do nothing else. Our position is wrong and untenable but it is not wise to keep an emotional people off balance.

"The Negroes have had 90 years of that sort of life and now they are winning it would take a lot of wisdom to say 'Go slow.' Perhaps it is too much to ask of them but it is for their own sake. I have known Negroes all my life and Negroes work my land for me. I know how they feel. But now I have people who say they are Negroes writing to me and saying 'You mean well for us but please hush. You mean good but you do harm.'"

Asked if a "go slow" would not cause ground already gained to be lost, Faulkner said:

"I don't know. I try to think of this in the longterm view. Now, I grant you that it is bad that there should be a minority people who because of their color don't have a right to social equality or to justice. But it is bad that Americans should be fighting Americans. That is what will happen because the Southern whites are back in the spirit of 1860. There could easily be another civil war and the South will be whipped again. My brother's son's a fairly intelligent man and he says 'If I have to die I'll die shooting niggrahs trying to get into a white school.' He's typical.

"In the long view, the Negro race will vanish in 300 years by inter-marriage. It's happened to every racial minority everywhere and it will happen here."

Q. What would be the best strategy for the liberals?

A. "Let the people stop a while. If that girl Autherine Lucy goes back to Alabama University on March 1st she will be killed. The NAACP should forget about Alabama University. They should send people now to the Universities of Georgia, Mississippi and South Carolina and let them be thrown out of each of those places too, until the white people of the South get so sick and tired of being harassed and worried they will have to do something about it. If they send that girl back to Tuscaloosa on March 1st she will be killed."

Q. Have you heard the reports of the arms buying in Tuscaloosa?

A. "Yes. If that girl dies, two or three white men will be killed, then eight or nine Negroes. Then the troops will come in. You know, we've never had race riots in the South before. They've had race riots in the North but in the South we just have persecution.

150

"The South is armed for revolt. After the Supreme Court decision [of 17 May 1954, on school integration] you couldn't get as much as a few rounds for a deer rifle in Mississippi. The gunsmiths were sold out. These white people will accept another civil war knowing they're going to lose. If the North knew the South they would know that this is not a theory or a moral convention which they are up against but a simple fact. I know people who've never fired a gun in their lives but who've bought rifles and ammunition."

Q. How long do you think it will be before the concrete aspects of discrimination—housing, employment, enfranchisement, education, social contacts—will have disappeared?

A. "In the Deep South, I don't know. As it was, in 15 years, the Negroes would have had good schools. Then came the decision of the Supreme Court and that will mean probably 20 years of trouble. I think that decision put the position of the Negro in the South back five years."

Q. Does that mean that you disapprove of the Court decree?

A. "I don't disapprove of it. It had to be promulgated and it just repeated what was said on January 3, 1863. If the white folks had given Negroes proper schools there would have been no need for the Court's decision."

Faulkner then restated the opinion which has divided him against the other Southern liberal writers:

"The Negro in the Deep South doesn't want to mix with the white man. He likes his own school, his own church. Segregation doesn't have to imply inferiority."

Asked "When your tenants tell you they prefer segregation, how do you know if they are talking to you as man to man and not as Southern Negro tenant to Southern white landlord?" Faulkner smiled and closed his eyes in thought but did not answer.

Q. How would you re-educate the Southern white to a different way of thinking?

A. "First of all, take off the pressure. Let him see just how untenable his position is. Let him see that people laugh at him. Just let him see how silly and foolish he looks. Give him time—don't force us. If that girl goes back to Tuscaloosa she will die: then the top will blow off. The government will send in its troops and we shall be back at

1860. They must stop pushing these people. The trouble is the North doesn't know that country. They don't know the South will go to war.

"Things have been getting better slowly for a long time. Only six Negroes were killed by whites in Mississippi last year, according to the police figures. The Supreme Court decree came 90 years too late. In 1863 it was a victory. In 1954 it was a tragedy. The same thing is happening in South Africa, in Algeria. People were too ignorant of their fellow-man and they realized his equality too late. This whole thing is not a confrontation of ideologies but of white folks against folks not white. It is worldwide. We must win the Indians, the Malayans, the 16 million Negro Americans and the rest to the white camp, make it worth their while."

Q. Apart from your advice to promising Southerners, white and black, to get their education out of the South, what would your advice to an ambitious Negro be?—To get out of the South altogether?

A. "No, he should stay in the South, where we need promising people, and be patient. Now is a time for calm, but that time will pass. The Negro has a right to equality. His equality is inevitable, an irresistible force, but as I see it you've got to take into consideration human nature which at times has nothing to do with moral truths. Truth says this and the fact says that. A wise person says 'Let's use this fact. Let's obliterate this fact first.' To oppose a material fact with a moral truth is silly."

Q. The Negroes of Montgomery, the capital of Alabama, have been boycotting the city's buses since December 5. Do you think this sort of passive resistance is a good idea?

A. "Yes, anything they do is good as long as they don't carry it too far. Today the white women of Montgomery have to go and fetch their Negro cooks by car. It is a good step, to let the white folks see that the world is looking on and laughing at them.

"But I don't like enforced integration any more than I like enforced segregation. If I have to choose between the United States government and Mississippi, then I'll choose Mississippi. What I'm trying to do now is not have to make that decision. As long as there's a middle road, all right, I'll be on it. But if it came to fighting I'd fight for Mississippi against the United States even if it meant going out into the street and shooting Negroes. After all I'm not going out to shoot Mississippians."

Q. You mean white Mississippians?

A. "No, I said Mississippians—in Mississippi the problem isn't racial. Ninety per cent of the Negroes are on one side with the whites, against a handful like me who believe that equality is important."

Q. Some of your remarks could be interpreted as disapproval of the existence of militant Negro defense organizations. How do you feel about the NAACP?

A. "That organization is necessary, but it must know when to let the opponent make the next move. Ninety years of oppression and injustice are there, but it is a lot for the white man to have to admit. It takes an extremely intelligent man to stop dead after 90 years of wrongdoing and the Southerner isn't that intelligent. He has to feel that what he is doing (when he reforms) is not being forced on him but is spontaneous. We have to make it so that he feels that he is being not just honest but generous. Give him time—right now it's emotional and he'll fight because the country's against him."

Q. In the European Press, "go slow" is criticized on the grounds that the susceptibilities of the persecuted deserve more consideration than the susceptibilities of the persecutor. How would you answer that criticism?

A. "The European critics are right, morally, but there is something stronger in man than a moral condition. Man will do certain things whether they be right or wrong. We know that racial discrimination is morally bad, that it stinks, that it shouldn't exist, but it does. Should we obliterate the persecutor by acting in a way that we know will send him to his guns, or should we compromise and let it work out in time and save whatever good remains in those white people?"

Q. If the position in the South was reversed and the Negroes formed a majority which had been persecuting and murdering a white minority for 90 years would you still say "Go slow" on reform?

A. "Yes. Yes, I would. But the way we see it in the South, the way I see it, is that the Negro is in a majority, because he has the country behind him. He could have the support of the federal army."

Q. Then you don't advise delays as an expedient because the Negro is numerically outnumbered by over two to one in the South?

A. "No. Take the case of Autherine Lucy. I say she shouldn't go back to Tuscaloosa not because she'll be one against a mob of 2000—

there'll be a hundred million Americans behind her—but because she'll get killed.

"The Negroes are right, make sure you've got that, they're right. But March 1st at Tuscaloosa is not a moral condition, it's a question of fact. I've always been on their (the Negroes') side, but if there's no middle ground, if people like me have got to choose then I'm on the side of Mississippi.

"I will go on saying that the Southerners are wrong and that their position is untenable but if I have to make the same choice Robert E. Lee made then I'll make it. My grandfather had slaves and he must have known that it was wrong but he fought in one of the first regiments raised by the Confederate Army, not in defense of his ethical position but to protect his native land from being invaded."

Q. Do you believe regional loyalty is a good quality?

A. "Well, you must believe in something."

Q. What about your belief in the principles expressed in your books?

A. "I shouldn't be betraying them. My Negro boys down on the plantation would fight against the North with me. If I say to them 'Go get your shotguns, boys,' they'll come."

Q. The churches are segregated in the South. Don't you think the churches could do much to improve the South by sticking to Christian principles?

A. "They could do much more but they are afraid to open their mouths. The Catholics have made a few moves. It is easier for the Catholics because they are Catholics first and members of the human race second."

Q. Is the basic cause of race prejudice economic, in your opinion?

A. "Absolutely. To produce cotton we have to have a system of peonage. That is absolutely what is at the bottom of the situation."

Q. Are the psychological rationalizations for prejudice something grafted on to the economic root?

A. "Yes. I would say that a planter who has a thousand acres wants to keep the Negro in a position of debt-peonage and in order to do it he is going to tell the poor class of white folks that the Negro is going to violate his daughter. But all he wants at the back of it is a system of peonage to produce his cotton at the highest rate of profit."

Q. Do you see the basic problem as one of education?

A. "Yes, whites and Negroes must be re-educated to the issue. The most important thing is good schools. The trouble is that Southern white people are not interested in schools. Only the Negro cares about education. If we had good schools we could get good teachers."

Q. Isn't it Utopian to hope for a high standard of schools in a rural community?

A. "Yes, it's a Utopian dream, but it must be a good dream because there's always been someone to dream it."

Q. Do you agree that the ambition-spur provided by persecution has made the Negro the potentially more capable of the two "races" in the South?

A. "Certainly. He's calmer, wiser, more stable than the white man. To have put up with this situation so long with so little violence shows a sort of greatness. Suppose two Negroes had murdered a white Emmett Till—there would have been a flood of emotionalism. The Negro rose above his anger. He knows that the problem (of his equality) will be solved because it must be. But these ignorant white people have got to be let alone so that they can think that they are changing on their own initiative.

"The poor white man knows that although the Negro can only buy the worst land, has bad tools and inferior livestock he can make a living better than white men could. With a little more social, economic and educational equality the Negro will often be the landlord and the white man will be working for him. And the Negro won't come out on top because of anything to do with the race but because he has always gotten by without scope—when they are given scope they use it fully. The Negro is trained to do more than a white man can with the same limitations.

"The vices that the Negro has have been created in him by the white man, by the system. He will make his own contribution to our society. Already his music and poetry have passed to the white man and what the white man has done with them is not Negro any more but something else.

"There is no such thing as an 'Anglo-Saxon' heritage and an African heritage. There is the heritage of man. Nothing is extinct in any race, only dormant. You are brave and tough when you have to be.

You are intelligent when the age demands it. There are all things in like degree in all races."

Q. How is it for a man like you to live in Mississippi?

A. "I get a lot of insulting and threatening letters and telephone calls, since I established my position [on this issue]. The tragic thing is that some of them come from Negroes, at least they say they're Negroes: it isn't just a solidarity of race—you get doctors and lawyers and preachers and newspaper editors and some Negroes too, all grouped against a few liberals like me. People phone up to threaten my life at three or four in the morning—they're usually drunk by then."

Q. Do you carry a gun?

A. "No. My friends say I ought to carry a pistol. But I don't think anyone will shoot me, it would cause too much of a stink. But the other liberals in my part of the country carry guns all the time."

(Author's note: This interview was taken from the typescript of a story that Howe, a reporter for the London Times, *sent to his newspaper in England. This was in fact never published at the time; the* Times *reduced the story, highlighting particular parts of it; in turn,* The Reporter, *a magazine in New York, reprinted the story with further abridgement; then* Time *magazine abridged it radically to two paragraphs. Faulkner sued for inaccuracy and libel, saying publicly that he was accused of saying things no sober man would say and no sane man believe. In the end, this was not contested. Howe's initial story was based on notes taken during the interview, which may explain two errors of fact Faulkner was unlikely to have made: his land was not a plantation but a much smaller farm [he called it Greenfield Farm; it was 13 miles east of Oxford] and his great-grandfather, not his grandfather, fought in the Civil War. I am grateful to Mr. Howe for supplying me with a copy of his original typescript.)*

Appendix IV: The Final McCaslin-Beauchamp-Edmonds Genealogy

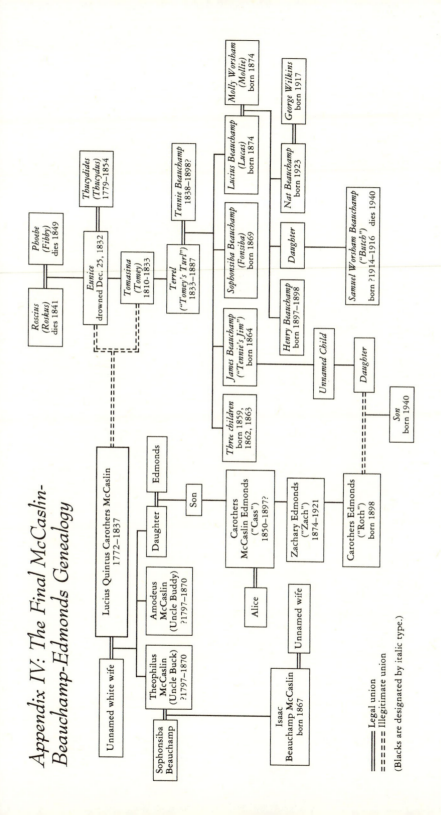

_____ Legal union

= = = = = Illegitimate union

(Blacks are designated by italic type.)

Notes and References

1. Lionel Trilling, "The McCaslins of Mississippi," *Nation*, 30 May 1942, 632, as quoted in *William Faulkner: The Critical Heritage*, ed. John Bassett (London: Routledge, 1975), 297–98.

2. Quoted in Joel Williamson, *William Faulkner and Southern History* (New York: Oxford University Press, 1993), 14.

3. Quoted in Drew Gilpin Faust, *Southern Stories: Slaveholders in Peace and War* (Columbia: University of Missouri Press, 1992), 29–30. She develops this at some length (30 ff).

4. The archetypal process is described by W. J. Cash in *The Mind of the South* (New York: Vintage, 1991), 14–17.

5. "Management of Negroes Upon Southern Estates / Rules and Regulations for the Government of a Southern Plantation, / by 'A Mississippi Planter'" in *Debow's Review* (New Orleans, June 1851), reprinted in Daniel Hoffman, *Faulkner's Country Matters: Folklore and Fable in Yoknapatawpha* (Baton Rouge: Louisiana State University Press, 1989), 153.

6. Quoted in Chalmers Archer, Jr., *Growing Up Black in Rural Mississippi: Memories of a Family, Heritage of a Place* (New York: Walker, 1992), 134.

7. Mr. Foby, "Management of Servants," *Southern Cultivator* 11 (August 1853): 226.

8. Herbert Shapiro, *White Violence and Black Response: From Reconstruction to Montgomery* (Amherst: University of Massachusetts Press, 1988), 223.

9. Hortense Powdermaker, *After Freedom* (New York: Viking, 1939); see 32, 33, 53, 54, 173, 174, 332, 335, 351.

10. W. E. B. DuBois, *The Souls of Black Folk* (1903), as quoted in Bertram Wyatt-Brown, "The Mask of Obedience," in *Society and Culture in the Slave South*, ed. J. William Harris (London: Routledge, 1992), 149.

11. V. S. Naipaul, *A Turn in the South* (New York: Vintage, 1989), 156.

12. Quoted by Wyatt-Brown in Harris (note 10), 142.

13. Richard Wright, *Black Boy: A Record of Childhood and Youth* (New York: Viking, 1966), 250.

14. For other documents on the history of the South pertaining to *Go Down, Moses*, see Arthur F. Kinney, *Critical Essays on William Faulkner: The McCaslin Family* (Boston: G. K. Hall, 1990), 8–22, 33–37.

15. For maps and further details, see Charles S. Aiken, "A Geographical Approach to William Faulkner's 'The Bear,'" *Geographical Review* 71:4 (October 1981): 446–59.

16. Other events fictionalized in *Go Down, Moses* are told by John B. Cullen, one of Faulkner's hunting partners, in collaboration with Floyd C. Watkins, in *Old Times in the Faulkner Country* (Chapel Hill: University of North Carolina Press, 1961).

17. Jim Faulkner, *Across the Creek: Faulkner Family Stories* (Jackson: University Press of Mississippi, 1986), 74.

18. Lewis M. Dabney, *The Indians of Yoknapatawpha: A Study in Literature and History* (Baton Rouge: Louisiana State University Press, 1974), 147–48.

19. See Elizabeth Meeks, *A Contextual Approach to the Teaching of Two Novels by William Faulkner at College Level* (D.Ed. diss., University of Houston, 1965), 107 ff.

20. Jack Case Wilson, *Faulkners, Fortunes, and Flames* (Nashville: Annadale Press, 1984), 27.

21. John Pilkington, *The Heart of Yoknapatawpha* (Jackson: University Press of Mississippi, 1981), 285–86.

22. George Marion O'Donnell, "Faulkner's Mythology," *Kenyon Review* (summer 1939): 1:285–99. The essay has frequently been reprinted; it is found, for example, in *William Faulkner: Four Decades of Criticism*, ed. Linda Welshimer Wagner ([East Lansing]: Michigan State University Press, 1973), 83–93.

23. Conrad Aiken, "William Faulkner: The Novel as Form," *Atlantic Monthly*, November 1939, 650–54. This essay has frequently been reprinted; see, for example, Wagner (note 22), 134–40 (quotation is on p. 136).

24. Warren Beck, "William Faulkner's Style," *American Prefaces* (spring 1941): 195–211. This essay has frequently been reprinted; see, for example, Wagner (note 22), 141–54. For important later discussions of Faulkner's style and its sources, see Beck, *Faulkner* (Madison: University of Wisconsin Press, 1976) and also Richard P. Adams, *Faulkner: Myth and Motion* (Princeton: Princeton University Press, 1968); Arthur F. Kinney, *Faulkner's Narrative Poetics: Style as Vision* (Amherst: University of Massachusetts Press, 1978);

Notes and References

Joseph W. Reed, Jr., *Faulkner's Narrative* (New Haven: Yale University Press, 1973); and Walter J. Slatoff, *Quest for Failure: A Study of William Faulkner* (Ithaca: Cornell University Press, 1960).

25. Trilling, in Bassett (note 1), 296–97.

26. Unsigned review, *Times Literary Supplement*, 10 October 1942, 497; reprinted in Bassett (note 1), 299–301 (quotation is on p. 300).

27. Malcolm Cowley, "William Faulkner's Legend of the South," *Sewanee Review* 53 (1945): 343–61. The essay is reprinted in Bassett (note 1), 301–13, from which I have drawn the quotations, which appear on pp. 304–5 and 307. The essay was later incorporated into the introduction to *The Portable Faulkner*, ed. Malcolm Cowley (New York: Viking, 1946), 1–24.

28. Robert Penn Warren, "Cowley's Faulkner," *New Republic* 115 (1946): 176–80, 234–37, reprinted in Bassett (note 1), 314–28 (quotation is on p. 315).

29. Ralph Ellison, "Twentieth-Century Fiction and the Black Mask of Humanity," *Confluence* 2 (1953): 3–21, reprinted in Bassett (note 1), 328–31 (reference to *Go Down, Moses* is on p. 330). The essay was later reprinted in Ellison's *Shadow and Act* (New York: Random House, 1964).

30. Both the Lewis and Perluck essays are reprinted in *Bear, Man, and God*, ed. Francis Lee Utley, Lynn Z. Bloom, and Arthur F. Kinney (New York: Random House, 1964); the Lewis essay is also reprinted in the second edition of that collection (1971).

31. Ursula Brumm, "Wilderness and Civilization: A Note on William Faulkner," *Partisan Review* 22:3 (1955): 340–50; excerpted in *Bear, Man, and God* (1971 ed.; see note 30), 251–52.

32. Olga W. Vickery, *The Novels of William Faulkner: A Critical Interpretation* (Baton Rouge: Louisiana State University Press, 1959), chap. 8, 124–34; see especially pp. 124–25.

33. Stanley Tick, "The Unity of *Go Down, Moses*," *Twentieth Century Literature* 8:2 (1962): 67–73, reprinted in Wagner (note 22), 327–34 (quotation is on p. 330).

34. Michael Millgate, *The Achievement of William Faulkner* (New York: Random House, 1963), 201–14; the treatment of the work as a novel begins on p. 203.

35. Thadious M. Davis, *Faulkner's "Negro": Art and the Southern Context* (Baton Rouge: Louisiana State University Press, 1983), 239–47; Walter Taylor, *Faulkner's Search for a South* (Urbana: University of Illinois Press, 1983), 118–44.

36. The term "wilderness trilogy," according to Matthews, was first coined by Arthur F. Kinney in "Faulkner and the Possibilities for Heroism," *Southern Review*, n.s., 6 (1970):1110–25, where its meaning is developed at some length.

37. Lyall H. Powers, *Faulkner's Yoknapatawpha Comedy* (Ann Arbor: University of Michigan Press, 1980), 169.

38. The exception is the publication in *Bear, Man, and God* (note 30). Although Faulkner prevented the separate publication of the five-part chapter in the last year of his life, Random House permitted its publication just after his death. Such permission was not granted again by his estate, to my knowledge. The late Albert Erskine, Faulkner's editor at Random House in 1962, gave the exceptional permission.

39. Ike's history is a peculiar one. He had minor roles earlier, in "A Bear Hunt" and "Lion," was a storekeeper in "Fool About a Horse," and was a farm owner in *The Hamlet*.

40. Sidney Kaplan, "The Miscegenation Issue in the Election of 1864," *Journal of Negro History* 34:3 (1949): 274–343.

41. Faust, *Southern Stories*, 65–69.

42. Thorpe's story is conveniently reprinted in both editions of *Bear, Man, and God* (note 30).

43. Grimwood's discussion of *Swallow Barn* is in his book *Heart in Conflict: Faulkner's Struggles with Vocation* (Athens: University of Georgia Press, 1987), 237–43.

44. All these materials are collected, some in excerpts, in *The Beauchamp Tragedy*, ed. Jules Zanger (Philadelphia: J. B. Lippincott Co., 1963). Poe's play, entitled *Politian* (1835), was left unfinished; Simms's novel was called *Beauchampe* (1842); and the story was used most recently in Warren's novel *World Enough and Time* (1950).

45. William Faulkner, "Sunset," in *William Faulkner: New Orleans Sketches*, ed. Carvel Collins (New York: Random House, 1958).

46. William Faulkner, "That Evening Sun," in *Collected Stories of William Faulkner* (New York: Random House, 1950).

47. Cornel West, *Race Matters* (Boston: Beacon Press, 1993), 100–101.

48. Peter Brooks, "Incredulous Narration: *Absalom, Absalom!*" *Comparative Literature* 34:3 (1982): 248.

49. Philip M. Weinstein, *Faulkner's Subject: A Cosmos No One Owns* (Cambridge: Cambridge University Press, 1992), 62.

Bibliography

Primary Sources

Novels (in order of composition)

Soldiers' Pay. New York: Liveright, 1970.

Mosquitoes. New York: Liveright, 1951.

Flags in the Dust. Edited by Douglas Day. New York: Random House, 1973. Originally abridged as *Sartoris* (New York: Random House, 1966).

The Sound and the Fury: The Corrected Text. New York: Vintage, 1990.

Sanctuary: The Original Text. New York: Random House, 1981.

As I Lay Dying. New York: Vintage, 1987.

Light in August. New York: Vintage, 1990.

Pylon. New York: Vintage, 1987.

Absalom, Absalom! The Corrected Text. New York: Vintage, 1990.

The Unvanquished. New York: Vintage, 1991.

The Wild Palms. New York: Vintage, 1964.

The Hamlet. 2d ed. New York: Random House, 1964.

Go Down, Moses. New York: Vintage, 1990. Original title: *Go Down, Moses and Other Stories* (New York: Random House, 1942).

Intruder in the Dust. New York: Vintage, 1993.

Requiem for a Nun. New York: Vintage, 1975.

A Fable. New York: Vintage, 1978.

The Town. New York: Vintage, 1961.

The Mansion. New York: Vintage, 1965.

The Reivers. New York: Vintage, 1966.

Collected Sketches and Stories

Big Woods. New York: Random House, 1955. Includes "A Bear Hunt" and excerpts of "The Bear" and "The Old People."

Collected Stories of William Faulkner. New York: Vintage, 1977. Includes "A Bear Hunt" and "A Justice," both of which touch on Sam Fathers's ancestry.

Knight's Gambit. New York: Vintage, 1978. Further stories about Gavin Stevens as a lawyer.

New Orleans Sketches. Edited by Carvel Collins. New York: Random House, 1968. Includes "Sunset."

Uncollected Stories of William Faulkner. Edited by Joseph Blotner. New York: Vintage, 1981. Includes "Lion," later incorporated into "The Bear"; early versions of "The Old People," "Pantaloon in Black," "The Bear," "Delta Autumn," and "Go Down, Moses"; and "A Point of Law" and "Gold Is Not Always," later incorporated into "The Fire and the Hearth." (Note: "Always," an early version of "Was," was never collected.)

Other Writings and Documents

Essays, Speeches & Public Letters. Edited by James B. Meriwether. New York: Random House, 1966. Includes important statements on race, such as "Letter to a Northern Editor," "On Fear: Deep South in Labor: Mississippi," "A Letter to the Negro Race," "Funeral Sermon for Mammy Caroline Barr," "Mississippi," "Address to the Southern Historical Association," "Address to the Raven, Jefferson, and ODK Societies of the University of Virginia," and several letters.

Faulkner in the University: Class Conferences at the University of Virginia, 1957–58. Edited (excerpted and transcribed) by Frederick L. Gwynn and Joseph L. Blotner. Charlottesville: University Press of Virginia, 1978.

Lion in the Garden: Interviews with William Faulkner, 1926–1962. Edited by James B. Meriwether and Michael Millgate. Lincoln: University of Nebraska Press, 1980. Includes Faulkner's most extended comments on his own writing.

Selected Letters of William Faulkner. Edited by Joseph Blotner. New York: Random House, 1977.

William Faulkner Manuscripts 16. Introduced and arranged by Thomas L. McHaney. 2 vols. New York: Garland, 1987. Reprints, with bibliographic essay, facsimiles of Faulkner's typescripts and miscellaneous typescript pages, typescript setting copy of the novel, and miscellaneous galley proofs.

Bibliography

Secondary Works

Biography

Blotner, Joseph. *Faulkner: A Biography*. 2 vols. New York: Random House, 1974. The most detailed and diplomatic biography.

———. *Faulkner: A Biography*. 1-vol. ed. New York: Random House, 1984. An abridgement of the original, with some new and corrected material; considerably more accessible.

Karl, Frederick R. *William Faulkner: American Writer*. New York: Weidenfeld & Nicolson, 1989. A fine psychoanalytic study.

Minter, David. *William Faulkner: His Life and Work*. Baltimore: Johns Hopkins University Press, 1980. A sensible joint reading of the author's life and fiction.

Williamson, Joel. *William Faulkner and Southern History*. New York: Oxford University Press, 1993. The most revealing family biography of the Falkner and Butler families (Faulkner's ancestors), as well as Faulkner himself, from a cultural perspective; especially informed and speculative on matters of class and race.

Wittenberg, Judith Bryant. *Faulkner: The Transfiguration of Biography*. Lincoln: University of Nebraska Press, 1979. A sensitive study of Faulkner's fiction as the "dark twin" of his life.

Bibliography

Bassett, John Earl. *William Faulkner: An Annotated Checklist of Criticism*. New York: Davis Lewis, 1972. Authoritative until 1970.

———. *Faulkner: An Annotated Checklist of Recent Criticism*. Kent, Ohio: Kent State University Press, 1983. Authoritative for the decade of the 1970s.

———. *Faulkner in the Eighties: An Annotated Critical Bibliography*. Metuchen, N.J.: Scarecrow Press, 1991. Authoritative for the 1980s.

McHaney, Thomas L. *William Faulkner: A Reference Guide*. Boston: G. K. Hall, 1976. A thorough and reliable work, now being updated.

Reference Tools

Bassett, John Earl, ed. *William Faulkner: The Critical Heritage*. London, Methuen, 1975. A history of Faulkner's influence and reputation, as well as his reception, through reviews and criticism published largely in his lifetime.

Brown, Calvin S. *A Glossary of Faulkner's South*. New Haven: Yale University Press, 1976. A reliable tool by a scholar who was Faulkner's friend and companion in Oxford, Mississippi.

Connolly, Thomas E. *Faulkner's World: A Directory of His People and Synopses of Actions in His Published Works.* Lanham, Md.: University Press of America, 1988. The best source for the publication history of *Go Down, Moses* and of each of its parts.

Gresset, Michel. *A Faulkner Chronology.* Translated by Arthur B. Scharff. Jackson: University Press of Mississippi, 1985. A chronological summary of important events in Faulkner's life and times.

Kinney, Arthur F., ed. *Critical Essays on William Faulkner: The McCaslin Family.* Boston: G. K. Hall, 1990. Includes important critical commentary on *Go Down, Moses*, a chronology, a genealogy, and cultural documents (e.g., accounts of the lynchings of Nelse Patton and Elwood Higginbotham).

Smith, Meredith. "A Chronology of *Go Down, Moses.*" *Mississippi Quarterly* 36:3 (summer 1983): 319–28.

Utley, Francis Lee, Lynn Z. Bloom, and Arthur F. Kinney, eds. *Bear, Man, and God: Eight Approaches to William Faulkner's "The Bear."* 2d ed. New York: Random House, 1971. An expanded and updated edition with important sections on cultural perspectives and race.

Volpe, Edmond L. *A Reader's Guide to William Faulkner.* New York: Farrar, Straus, & Giroux, 1964. A reliable critical reading of *Go Down, Moses* (230–52), chronology (393–96), and genealogical chart (231).

Books

Backman, Melvin. *Faulkner: The Major Years: A Critical Study.* Bloomington: Indiana University Press, 1966. An astute early appraisal arguing that *Go Down, Moses* is about the deprivation of family love and the shame and grief caused for whites and blacks (160–74).

Brooks, Cleanth. *William Faulkner: First Encounters.* New Haven: Yale University Press, 1983. A richer revisionary reading of *Go Down, Moses* (129–59), compared with his *William Faulkner: The Yoknapatawpha Country* (1963), by a sensitive and knowledgeable Southerner.

Creighton, Joanne V. *William Faulkner's Craft of Revision.* Detroit: Wayne State University Press, 1977. A thorough study of various drafts of *Go Down, Moses* (85–148) as they form a "short story composite" with chapters both autonomous and integrated.

Early, James. *The Making of "Go Down, Moses."* Dallas: Southern Methodist University Press, 1972. A very accessible study of the development of the novel; especially strong on part 4 of "The Bear." Omits "Pantaloon in Black."

Fowler, Doreen, and Ann J. Abadie, eds. *Faulkner and Race: Faulkner and Yoknapatawpha, 1986.* Jackson: University Press of Mississippi, 1987. An impressive collection with important ideas by every contributor; see especially Jackson, Davis, Rhodes, Taylor, Polk, Weinstein, Perkins, Chakovsky, and Grimwood.

Bibliography

Grimwood, Michael. *Heart in Conflict: Faulkner's Struggles with Vocation*. Athens: University of Georgia Press, 1987. An acutely informed study of the pressures and influences on the composition of *Go Down, Moses*; especially strong on "Delta Autumn."

Hoffman, Daniel. *Faulkner's Country Matters: Folklore and Fable in Yoknapatawpha*. Baton Rouge: Louisiana State University Press, 1989. Valuable as a poet's felt observations on cultural values and narrative technique (107–74); strongest on "Was" and "The Old People."

Hunt, John W. *William Faulkner: Art in Theological Tension*. Syracuse, N.Y.: Syracuse University Press, 1965. An astute discussion of differing epistemological and theological positions in "The Bear" (137–68).

Jehlen, Myra. *Class and Character in Faulkner's South*. New York: Columbia University Press, 1976. A tough examination of race, proposing that despite intentions and actions, a conservative separateness of races is the best Faulkner can discover in *Go Down, Moses* (97–124).

King, Richard H. *A Southern Renaissance: The Cultural Reawakening of the American South, 1930–1955*. New York: Oxford University Press, 1980. A broad historical study of the period about which Faulkner wrote; chapter 6 reads *Go Down, Moses* as family history informed on occasion by Faulkner's own history.

Kinney, Arthur F. *Faulkner's Narrative Poetics: Style as Vision*. Amherst: University of Massachusetts Press, 1978. Argues that the reader's understanding of *Go Down, Moses* depends on an inclusive appreciation of all the novel's events, beginning with but surpassing Ike's (215–41).

Kuyk, Dirk, Jr. *Threads Cable-Strong: William Faulkner's "Go Down, Moses."* Lewisburg, Penn.: Bucknell University Press, 1983. A microscopically precise and persistently schematic reading of the novel that occasions some insights (regarding Sam and Ike and the wilderness) and offers some aberrant interpretations (Rider as fantastic, Molly as a seer), usually at the cost of flexibility and imagination.

Levins, Lynn Gartrell. *Faulkner's Heroic Design: The Yoknapatawpha Novels*. Athens: University of Georgia Press, 1976. A close reading of "The Bear" from the perspective of Genesis (75–94).

Matthews, John T. *The Play of Faulkner's Language*. Ithaca, N.Y.: Cornell University Press, 1982. A richly articulated reading of *Go Down, Moses* that examines the inarticulation and erasures in its various rites of mourning (212–73).

Moreland, Richard C. *Faulkner and Modernism: Rereading and Rewriting*. Madison: University of Wisconsin Press, 1990. A subtle but deeply rewarding study of the limitations of discourse due to the shame of the dominant race and the marginalization of blacks and women as seen in *Go Down, Moses* (156–93).

Peavy, Charles D. *Go Slow Now: Faulkner and the Race Question*. Eugene: University of Oregon Books, 1971. The best and most succinct compilation of Faulkner's public thoughts on racial problems in the South after *Go Down, Moses* (with commentary).

Pikoulis, John. *The Art of William Faulkner*. Totowa, N.J.: Barnes and Noble, 1982. Contends that the "debilitating pretensions" and lack of love and responsibility of white settlers promote, in *Go Down, Moses*, a radical division that allows only antagonistic respect or exploitation until Ike displaces these with Keatsian imagery (192–226).

Snead, James A. *Figures of Division: William Faulkner's Major Novels*. New York: Methuen, 1986. A theoretically sophisticated reading of *Go Down, Moses*, showing that present divisions of time, class, and race urge a search for origin and unity; maintains that such attempts fail because "*histoire* diverges radically from *récit*" (180–211).

Sundquist, Eric J. *Faulkner: The House Divided*. Baltimore: Johns Hopkins University Press, 1983. Arguably the most penetrating analysis of *Go Down, Moses*, proposing that Ike's repudiation and Lucas's moral ascendancy, linking hunting and miscegenation, are paradoxically only able to honor love at the moment of its denial or destruction (131–59).

Taylor, Walter. *Faulkner's Search for a South*. Urbana: University of Illinois Press, 1983. Drawing on Faulkner's life, other works, and Southern mores, Taylor provides an eloquent reading of *Go Down, Moses* as Faulkner's most earnest effort to penetrate the consequences of slavery.

Warren, Robert Penn. *Segregation: The Inner Conflict in the South*. New York: Random House, 1956. Useful as a contemporary nonfiction account, by another major white Southern novelist, of the Southerner's understanding of race in the years following *Go Down, Moses*.

Wright, Richard. *Native Son*. New York: Library of America, 1991. A Mississippi black novelist's account of black life, published the same year as Faulkner's "Pantaloon in Black"; the basis for an instructive comparison.

Young, Stark. *So Red the Rose*. With a preface by George Garrett. Nashville, Tenn.: J. S. Sanders, 1992. The most critically acclaimed best-seller in the 1930s, by Faulkner's fellow writer in Oxford. A novel of family life and conflict on antebellum Mississippi plantations, based on family papers and documents.

Zender, Karl F. *The Crossing of the Ways: William Faulkner, the South, and the Modern World*. New Brunswick, N.J.: Rutgers University Press, 1989. Sees Roth and Lucas in *Go Down, Moses* as Faulkner's own exploratory self-portraits, with modifications (73–84).

Articles

Aiken, Conrad. "William Faulkner: The Novel as Form." *Atlantic Monthly* 164 (November 1939): 650–54. This classic essay, still valuable, argues

Bibliography

that Faulkner's presentation depends on "immersion" and "deliberately withheld meaning."

Anderson, Carl L. "Faulkner's 'Was': 'A Deadlier Purpose Than Simple Pleasure.'" *American Literature* 61:3 (October 1989): 414–28. A useful explication of the poker games in "Was" and of the early differentiation of Uncle Buck and Uncle Buddy.

Baldwin, James, "Faulkner and Desegregation." In *Nobody Knows My Name*, 117–26. New York: Vintage, 1993. A forceful response to Faulkner's ideas on race at the close of *Go Down, Moses* and his subsequent public statements.

Barker, Stephen. "From Old Gold to I.O.U.'s: Ike McCaslin's Debased Genealogical Coin." *Faulkner Journal* 3:1 (fall 1987): 2–25. Looks at Ike's need for self-identification in "The Bear" and his failure to find the appropriate means.

Bluestein, Gene. "Faulkner and Miscegenation." *Arizona Quarterly* 45:2 (summer 1987): 151–64. Uses scientific data to judge Faulkner's use of miscegenation in his works.

Canfield, J. Douglas. "Faulkner's Grecian Urn and Ike McCaslin's Empty Legacies." *Arizona Quarterly* 36:4 (winter 1980): 359–84. A lively and provocative essay on the empty myths left to Ike by his progenitors (both McCaslins and Beauchamps) and his responses.

Clarke, Graham. "Marking Out and Digging In: Language as Ritual in *Go Down, Moses*." In *William Faulkner: The Yoknapatawpha Fiction*, edited by Robert Lee, 147–64. New York: St. Martin's Press, 1990. A speculative reading of the novel as a depiction of the Southern version of the American Dream, emphasizing the importance of the geographical elements of wilderness, delta, and river.

Cowley, Malcolm. Introduction to *The Portable Faulkner*, edited by Cowley, 1–24. New York: Viking, 1946. Although sometimes superseded, this remains a good overview of Faulkner's work; it had Faulkner's approval at the time of its writing.

Dunn, Margaret M. "The Illusion of Freedom in *The Hamlet* and *Go Down, Moses*." *American Literature* 57:3 (October 1985): 407–23. A surprisingly fruitful juxtaposition showing the complicated sense of freedom in both works.

Klotz, Marvin. "Procrustean Revision in *Go Down, Moses*." *American Literature* 37:1 (March 1965): 1–16. Unlike Grimwood, Klotz argues that the short stories written first for the magazine market are often badly joined and inconsistent when incorporated into *Go Down, Moses*.

Lewis, R. W. B. "The Hero in the New World: William Faulkner's 'The Bear.'" *Kenyon Review* 13:4 (autumn 1951): 641–60. Condensed and revised in *The Picaresque Saint* (New York: J. B. Lippincott, 1961), 193–209. A classic essay and the most positive view of Ike. Sees "The

Bear" as "a canticle or chant relating the birth, the baptism"—the descent into darkness and regeneration, even "incarnation"—of Isaac.

Lydenberg, John. "Nature Myth in Faulkner's 'The Bear.'" *American Literature* 24:1 (March 1952): 62–72. The classic essay on "The Bear" (without part 4) as a primitive nature myth.

Mackethan, Lucinda H. "Plantation Fiction 1865–1900," in *The History of Southern Literature*, ed. Louis Rubin et al (Baton Rouge: Louisiana State University Press, 1895). A discussion of some of Faulkner's antecedents among Southern writers (pp. 209–18).

McGee, Patrick. "Gender and Generation in Faulkner's 'The Bear.'" *Faulkner Journal* 1:1 (fall 1985): 46–54. Compares our reading of signs and traces in "The Bear" with Ike's readings and willful repressions.

McMillen, Neil R. and Noel Polk, "Faulkner on Lynching," in *The Faulkner Journal* 8:1 (Fall 1992): 3–13.

Michelsen, David. "The Campfire and the Hearth in *Go Down, Moses.*" *Mississippi Quarterly* 38:3 (summer 1985): 311–27. A structuralist reading of the novel that sees heart/home/cooperative intimacy versus hunt/games/competition as the calculus for understanding it.

O'Donnell, George Marion. "Faulkner's Mythology." *Kenyon Review* 1:3 (summer 1939): 285–99. A classic overview of Faulkner's canon, on the eve of the publication of *Go Down, Moses*, as an exploration of the conflict between the Sartorises and the Snopses, the landed aristocracy and the poor whites.

Perluck, Herbert A. "'The Heart's Driving Complexity': An Unromantic Reading of Faulkner's 'The Bear.'" *Accent* 20 (winter 1960): 23–46. Sees "The Bear" as a parable of pride and evil; views the "romantic" reading of events as "a Christian pastoral of redemption" as Ike's willful misinterpretation.

Ragan, David Paul. "The Evolution of Roth Edmonds in *Go Down, Moses.*" *Mississippi Quarterly* 38:3 (summer 1985): 295–309. A very useful guide to the development of Roth, through the early stories and the later novel, as a crucial connection between Lucas and Ike.

Simpson, Lewis P. "Ike McCaslin and the Second Fall of Man." In *Bear, Man, and God: Eight Approaches to William Faulkner's "The Bear,"* edited by Francis Lee Utley, Lynn Z. Bloom, and Arthur F. Kinney, 202–9. New York: Random House, 1971. Isaac McCaslin of "The Bear" is seen as a fallen hero in an industrial age.

Taylor, Walter. "'Pantaloon': The Negro Anomaly at the Heart of *Go Down, Moses.*" *American Literature* 44:3 (October 1972): 430–44. Examines Faulkner's "failed" portrait of Rider, viewed as the intended corrective to Ike's excessive praise and misconstruction of blacks in the novel.

Bibliography

Tick, Stanley. "The Unity of *Go Down, Moses*." *Twentieth Century Literature* 8:2 (July 1962): 63–73. An early but still authoritative essay arguing that "no section [of the novel] is fully autonomous."

Utley, Francis Lee. "Pride and Humility: The Cultural Roots of Ike McCaslin." In *Bear, Man, and God*, 167–87. The classic anthropological and folkloristic reading of "The Bear," comprehensive in scope.

Warren, Robert Penn. "Faulkner: The South and the Negro." *Southern Review*, n.s., 1:3 (summer 1965): 501–29. Warren's classic statement on Faulkner's body of work, focusing near the end on *Go Down, Moses*; first presented as an address at the University of Mississippi, Oxford, in April 1965, shortly after Faulkner's death.

Willis, Susan. "Aesthetics of the Rural Slum: Contradictions and Dependency in 'The Bear.'" *Social Text 2* (summer 1979): 82–103. Contends that the wilderness and commissary in "The Bear" encode the historical opposition between the plantation system and industrial capitalism—a radical disunity that myth and mediation attempt to reconcile.

Zender, Karl F. "Reading in 'The Bear.'" *Faulkner Studies* 1 (1980): 91–99. The way Ike studies the ledgers in "The Bear" can instruct us on how to read *Go Down, Moses*—by repetition, through which overlooked and subordinate details take on sense and significance.

History

Campbell, Will D. *Providence*. Atlanta, Ga.: Longstreet Press, 1992. One man's account, from oral and written testimony, of the history of one square mile in Holmes County, Mississippi, near Faulkner's own county, from the cession of the Choctaws to the present; the comparison with *Go Down, Moses* is surprisingly instructive. The source for epigraphs to chapters 5, 6, and 7 of this volume.

Cash, W. J. *The Mind of the South*. Introduction by Bertram Wyatt-Brown. New York: Vintage, 1991. This classic work, now a half century old, is still seminal; revolutionary at the time, Cash's portrayal of the social and economic history of the South is frequently the basis of current thought and work. See also *The Mind of the South Fifty Years Later*, edited by Charles W. Eagles (Jackson: University Press of Mississippi, 1992).

Dollard, John. *Caste and Class in a Southern Town*, 3d ed. Garden City, N.Y.: Doubleday Anchor, 1957. A widely influential work of social psychology, using interviews in "Southerntown" (Indianola, Mississippi, 100 miles southwest of Oxford). The chapters on race provide fundamental context for understanding Rider, Lucas, and Butch Beauchamp.

Eaton, Clement. *The Mind of the Old South*, rev. ed. Baton Rouge: Louisiana State University Press, 1967. Archetypal biographies.

Stowe, Steven M. *Intimacy and Power in the Old South: Ritual in the Lives of the Planters*. Baltimore: Johns Hopkins University Press, 1987. Discusses, with theory and example, the antebellum rituals of honor, courtship, and coming of age—providing a rich context for understanding Zack and Lucas, Sophonsiba and Uncle Buck, and young Isaac McCaslin, respectively.

Taylor, William R. *Cavalier and Yankee: The Old South and American National Character*. New York: George Braziller, 1961. The classic examination of the Cavalier mentality and practices that served as the basis for the culture in which McCaslin founded his plantation.

Woodward, C. Vann. *The Burden of Southern History*, rev. ed. Baton Rouge: Louisiana State University Press, 1970. A retrospective collection of essays by the leading historian of the South, attempting to define "Southern identity" by means of political, social, and literary history.

Wyatt-Brown, Bertram. *Southern Honor: Ethics and Behavior in the Old South*. New York: Oxford University Press, 1982. A fundamental analysis of the code of honor, taken from the Old World to the Old South, that informs the behavior of several generations of the McCaslin family—both those who accept that code and those who oppose its customs.

Race

Bennett, Lerone, Jr. *Before the Mayflower: A History of Black America*, 6th ed. New York: Penguin, 1993. A highly readable and deeply moving history contextualizing Faulkner's Mississippi and *Go Down, Moses* from the blacks' perspective. Includes a detailed chronology of events.

Genovese, Eugene D. *Roll, Jordan, Roll: The World the Slaves Made*. New York: Vintage, 1976. A masterly history of slavery from the perspective of a white Marxist. Sometimes facile in his generalizations, Genovese nevertheless discusses paternalism and miscegenation in ways pointedly helpful in understanding L. Q. C. McCaslin, Uncle Buck and Uncle Buddy, and Hubert Beauchamp. His analyses of the notions of accommodation and resistance are helpful in understanding Lucas and Percival Brownlee.

Harris, J. William, ed. *Society and Culture in the Slave South*. London: Routledge, 1992. Arguably an indispensable anthology recording the present state of thought on all aspects of cultural life; serves as an excellent starting place for studying the McCaslin, Beauchamp, and Edmonds families.

Litwack, Leon F. *Been in the Storm So Long: The Aftermath of Slavery*. New York: Vintage, 1980. A detailed history of blacks just after the Civil War in the South; the middle chapters especially help in understanding Zack and Cass, as well as Lucas's and Molly's positions on the McCaslin plantation.

Bibliography

McGovern, James R. *Anatomy of a Lynching: The Killing of Claude Neal*. Baton Rouge: Louisiana State University Press, 1982. This thorough historical and sociological study of a Florida lynching in 1934 can provide a broad background to Rider's sense of race relations and supply a model for events surrounding his killing.

McMillen, Neil R. *Dark Journey: Black Mississippians in the Age of Jim Crow*. Urbana: University of Illinois Press, 1990. An inclusive view of black life in Mississippi from 1890 to 1940. Sheds light on the occupations and possibilities of Rider, Lucas, and Molly; also helpful in understanding George Wilkins and Nat.

Silver, James W. *Mississippi: The Closed Society*, new, enlarged ed. New York: Harcourt Brace, and World, 1966. Faulkner's close friend in the civil rights movement, a history professor at the University of Mississippi in Oxford, gives a personal account of racial protests over the admission of a black student to "Ole Miss" three months after Faulkner's death.

Williamson, Joel. *The Crucible of Race: Black-White Relations in the American South since Emancipation*. New York: Oxford University Press, 1984. A detailed and reliable history of race in the South in the twentieth century, beginning with census records. Also published in an abridged form as *A Rage for Order* (New York: Oxford University Press, 1986).

Index

Index

Index

Index

The Author

Arthur F. Kinney has taught at the University of Michigan, Yale University, and Clark University; he is presently Thomas W. Copeland Professor of Literary History at the University of Massachusetts, Amherst, and Adjunct Professor of English at New York University. He is the author of *Faulkner's Narrative Poetics: Style as Vision* (1978); coeditor of *Bear, Man, and God: Eight Approaches to William Faulkner's "The Bear"* (1963; revised 1971), with Francis Lee Utley and Lynn Z. Bloom, and *Approaches to Teaching "The Sound and the Fury"* (forthcoming from Modern Language Association of America), with Stephen Hahn; and the editor of a five-volume series on Faulkner's families (*Critical Essays on William Faulkner: The McCaslin Family*, the third in the series, was published in 1990. *The Sutpen Family* is forthcoming in 1996). The recipient of major fellowships, he has lectured widely on Faulkner in Europe and the United States. His inaugural public lecture as a Fulbright Fellow at Oxford University, "Form and Function in *Absalom, Absalom!*," was published in *Southern Review* (n.s., 14:4 [October 1978]: 677–91).